*There is always a pleasure in unravelling a mystery,
in catching at the gossamer clue
which will guide to certainty.*

—19th-CENTURY AUTHOR ELIZABETH GASKELL

LOVE'S A MYSTERY

Love's a Mystery in Sleepy Hollow, New York
Love's a Mystery in Cape Disappointment, Washington
Love's a Mystery in Cut and Shoot, Texas
Love's a Mystery in Nameless, Tennessee
Love's a Mystery in Hazardville, Connecticut
Love's a Mystery in Deadwood, Oregon
Love's a Mystery in Gnaw Bone, Indiana
Love's a Mystery in Tombstone, Arizona
Love's a Mystery in Peculiar, Missouri
Love's a Mystery in Crooksville, Ohio
Love's a Mystery in Last Chance, Iowa
Love's a Mystery in Panic, Pennsylvania
Love's a Mystery in Embarrass, Wisconsin

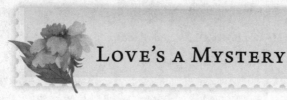

LOVE'S A MYSTERY

in

EMBARRASS
WI

BECKY MELBY &
CYNTHIA RUCHTI

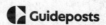

Love's a Mystery is a trademark of Guideposts.

Published by Guideposts Books & Inspirational Media
100 Reserve Road, Suite E200
Danbury, CT 06810
Guideposts.org

Cover and interior design by Müllerhaus
Cover illustration by Dan Burr at Illustration Online LLC.
Typeset by Aptara, Inc.

ISBN 978-1-959634-42-3 (hardcover)
ISBN 978-1-959634-41-6 (epub)
ISBN 978-1-959634-40-9 (epdf)

Printed and bound in the United States of America
10 9 8 7 6 5 4 3 2 1

AT FIRST BLUSH

by

BECKY MELBY

"He that answereth a matter before he heareth it,
it is folly and shame unto him."

—PROVERBS 18:13 (KJV)

∾ CHAPTER ONE ∾

Embarrass, Wisconsin
December 1, 1901

Lilly Galloway set perfectly plated pieces of coffee-chocolate chess pie in front of three of the Galloway Hotel's Sunday regulars then held her breath, waiting for a nod or scowl from the shortest man. Chef Jean-Claude Pascal chewed and swallowed then poked at the sugared crust with his fork. Finally, when Lilly thought her lungs might burst, a smile tipped one side of his moustache. "*Magnifique,* as always."

Lilly inhaled then turned to the tall, skinny member of the trio. "How are things at the camp, Jimmie? Everything on schedule for the season?"

Jimmie fiddled with the red bandanna knotted below his Adam's apple. "Not if you ask Lamoreaux."

She willed away the blush the name triggered. "He's always a bit anxious right before logging starts."

"Yep. More so this year on account of our numbers are down. But don't you worry, me and Axe ain't goin' nowhere. Your pies and this little Frenchman's grub will keep the both of us here until some dandy sweeps you off your feet and carries you back to the city."

A picture flashed in her mind of a clean-shaven man with slicked hair and an ascot tie throwing her over his shoulder and carting her back to Milwaukee. She wanted neither the dandy nor the city. She laughed and turned to the older, thickset man known as Axe. "How many years have you been a sawyer?"

"Far too many. Time to look for a job that pays more and doesn't threaten to kill me every time I turn my back." He tapped the folded newspaper at his right elbow. "Might just take up kidnapping. It's been almost a year since that boy went missing in Omaha. The kidnapper got twenty-five grand, returned the kid, and never got caught."

Lilly shook her head. "I'll bake you a special loaf of bread when I come visit you in prison."

Axe's laugh rumbled across the table. "Knew I could count on you."

"Kidnappin' is too complicated. Train robbin' is the way to go." Jimmie's scraggly moustache wobbled as he grinned. "Those guys who got the money box last month are still dodgin' the law."

Lilly rolled her eyes. "You two enjoy planning your next big crime, but some of us need to make an honest living, so I will bid you adieu." She returned to the kitchen.

While she didn't mind waiting on tables, the kitchen was the place where she felt she was doing what God had gifted her to do. After washing her hands, she finished fluting the crust on the seventh pie she'd made that morning and began the part she enjoyed the most.

Scooping up the scraps of dough she'd trimmed, she squished them into a ball then rolled it out flat. In a gesture she could do in her sleep now, she swished the tip of a paring knife in four arcs, making two half circles on each side, then added two antennae sprouting from the top. With practiced care, she lifted the butterfly cutout and placed it in the center of the lumpy pie bulging with apple slices.

"There's no time for that frivolous frippery today." The comment came on an irritated sigh. Bette, Lilly's half sister, leaned on the doorframe, nodding her head toward the dining room. Still wearing her church dress, she looked far too stylish to be waiting on tables. Bette raised an arm and dabbed her forehead with her sleeve. "Sunday crowd's bigger than usual, and the loggers are in rare form. Better make more chocolate and another cherry while you're at it, or you'll not have enough to send back with Jean-Claude. And have you thought ahead to order enough baking supplies for Christmas? We could get snow any day and the train might not…"

As Bette rambled on, Lilly heard a soft *tsk* behind her. Dottie, their cook, the little round woman who woke before the sun every morning to fry rashers of bacon and dozens of eggs while prepping sides of beef and whole chickens for the dinner and supper crowds, never tried too hard to hide her dislike of the way Bette treated Lilly. Her quick wit had saved Lilly's outlook on more days than she could possibly count.

Repressing a smile triggered by that one little syllable uttered by Dottie, Lilly cut six slits fanning out from her "frivolous frippery." She sprinkled the top with sugar and slid the pie onto the middle rack of the cookstove. After closing the oven door and checking the fire, she bent down, reached into a barrel, and filled her apron with green apples, enough for two Dutch apple pies. Listening to Dottie sing "Rock of Ages" while mapping out her next few steps… *make enough dough for eight crusts, drain the cherries, brew coffee, mix the cocoa and sugar…*kept her thoughts from falling into Bette's Slough of Despond.

If Bette had her way, she'd turn the Closed sign over for the last time and hop a train back to Milwaukee in a heartbeat. Lilly didn't share her sister's longing to return to "decorum and civility." She'd been sixteen in 1895 when her parents died of smallpox and Bette had insisted she come north to live with her, practically a stranger though they shared the same blood. Some of it, anyway.

She and Bette had the same father, but different mothers. Bette's mother had died when she was twelve. Two years later, her father had remarried, and a year after that, Lilly was born. She and Bette had only lived under the same roof for four years before Bette moved to the tiny village of Embarrass to start a hotel with her intended. Sadly, the man Bette was promised to had been killed in a logging accident two weeks before their wedding and only days before he was to quit logging for the safe role of a hotelier. As if grief were not enough of a burden to bear, Thomas had left the hotel to Bette. Along with its mortgage.

Bette was stuck—in a town whose name meant the same thing. Though travelers assumed something scandalous or humorous had occurred in the little river town, the French word *embarrasser* meant not only "to embarrass." It also meant "to obstruct." The river on which the village sat was often choked with logs during the spring season, causing the French-Canadian lumberjacks to coin the name *Riviére d'Embarras*. English settlers had modified the name, and the town and the river had been known as Embarrass ever since.

While Lilly did have some fond memories of school friends, attending teas with her mother, and downtown shopping trips, she'd always been a nature lover, preferring to spend time in the small woods behind their modest Milwaukee home. Here, in the expansive Northwoods, she could ignore her sister's reprimands about what constituted "appropriate behavior" for a young woman. Here, no one batted an eye when she donned breeches to ride horseback or wandered in the forest with a butterfly net.

Recently, she had tried to take Bette's instructions a bit more seriously...for one reason alone. A tall, broad-shouldered, witty, sky-blue-eyed reason. Not that it did any good. No matter what she wore, how she fixed her hair, how she smiled, fawned, or fluttered her eyelashes, Élan Lamoreaux still saw her as the gangly sixteen-year-old city girl she'd been when they first met. The foreman of the *Soleil Rouge* lumber camp was as dense as the century-old white pines he felled.

And...he was here. Now.

Peering through the half-open kitchen door, Lilly stared down the long hallway at the man who stood in the foyer blocking the light from the window in the front door. Like the giant woodsman in the French-Canadian lumbermen's tall tales, the one whose footsteps created the thousands of lakes in Wisconsin and Minnesota, he was larger than life and stronger than any other two men put together. At least in her mind, he was.

He took a few steps, his gaze sweeping the dining room. She held her breath, wondering if he sought her. And then he waved. Her heart thudded against her ribs. Clutching her apron with her left hand, she raised her right hand in a shaky greeting...as Élan joined Axe, Jimmie, and Jean-Claude, whose hands were raised just like hers. Mortified, and hoping he hadn't seen her wave, she dropped her hand. At the last second, before picking up his menu, he looked her way. And winked.

A dozen green apples tumbled onto the plank floor, rolling under the stove and the table. And out the partially open door into the dining room.

Lilly sank to her knees as a single, determined apple kept rolling. And rolling. Stopping under a table. An inch from Élan's boots.

Jimmie and Axe guffawed.

Her face burned. Her pulse slammed against her eardrums the way she wanted to bang her head against the wall. Head down, she concentrated on picking up apples, counting them under her breath, as if her focused attention would make it look like she hadn't noticed the wayward fruit. Maybe he hadn't either. Maybe—

"I believe you dropped this, *Papillon*."

That name. The one only he called her. French for butterfly. It had the same effect as his wink, discombobulating her senses.

"Thanks, M-moose." Using the English translation of his name, the nickname she'd given him years ago, made her appear casual, unflustered. Didn't it? As if it was an everyday occurrence to be kneeling in her kitchen at the feet of the most handsome man in all of Wisconsin. A man who had just winked at her.

Slowly, she lifted her blazing face, up and up, until she met those sky-blue eyes. Eyes that danced with mirth.

She couldn't let him see her turning into a puddle of warm molasses at his feet. With a bracing breath for courage, she stood. Too fast. The kitchen tilted. A large hand grabbed her upper arm, steadying her.

"Are you all right?"

No. No, no, no. Not even close to being all right. But she wasn't about to let him see her swooning like a schoolgirl. "Just stood up too fast." She tried to snatch the apple from the hand that wasn't still gripping her arm, but he wouldn't let go. "I'm f-fine." Her lips didn't seem to want to do what her brain told them to.

"Maybe you need to eat something." Grinning, he lifted the apple to her lips.

Behind him, Bette cleared her throat, and Élan lowered the apple and flattened against the doorframe.

"Excuse me, Mr. Lamoreaux." Bette pushed past him with a glare that threatened to bring on a blizzard a month early. "I have the same rules in my kitchen as you have in your camp. No unauthorized persons in the work area." Turning, she simply said, "Lilly." The one-word warning conveyed paragraphs. Paragraphs she'd likely hear over supper. *When the dining room is open, we do nothing but work. We do not fraternize with the customers, especially the loggers. You must do nothing to convey the wrong impression.*

Lilly grabbed the apple. This time he let go of it. With a nod and another wink, Moose turned and walked away.

He'd *winked*. Twice. She couldn't remember him ever doing that before. What did it mean? People winked at children who did something childishly entertaining. Was that it? Was he simply laughing at her clumsiness? Men winked at women for many reasons, many of them wrong reasons. But Élan, for all his burly roughness, was a gentleman.

So what did it mean? As she peeled more apples, mixed enough topping for three Dutch apple pies, and drained two quarts of cherries in cheesecloth, her overactive mind pondered the winks. Lost in thought, she was stirring ingredients for two coffee-chocolate chess pies, a recipe she'd created herself, when another shadow blocked the light in the kitchen doorway. Well, some of the light.

Lilly grinned as the lumber camp chef, Chef Jean-Claude Pascal, all five-foot-four of him, stepped into the kitchen. At her insistence, and over Bette's protests, Jean-Claude had been deemed an "authorized" person. This little man, old enough to be her father, had been her first friend when she moved to this tiny wilderness town. Their friendship had started the day she served her first pie to hotel guests. He'd come storming into the kitchen, shouting in French, *"Madame, on mange d'abord avec les yeux."* It meant "Madam, we eat with our eyes first!" Though humiliated when he'd stuck the hastily dished plate of blueberry pie under her nose, it was a phrase she had come to adore. *Présentation*, as Jean-Claude so often exclaimed, was everything. It was he who had encouraged her to create her own "signature in pie crust"—her butterfly cutouts.

Jean-Claude greeted her as he always did, with a kiss on the cheek. "How are things in the kitchen of ze famous Lilly Galloway?" He reached for a clean silver spoon, dipped it in the crumbly flour, sugar, and butter Dutch apple topping, and tasted, pulling the spoon slowly from his lips.

Once again, Lilly wondered if she'd be rewarded with a smile or an opportunity to learn something new.

"Délicieux." Jean-Claude pressed his thumb and forefinger together and kissed them with a loud smack. "Someone has taught you well."

He set the spoon on the table and watched as she stirred the ingredients for the chess pie just the way he'd taught her, with "vigor but not haste."

"It has been a busy morning. I have seven pies for you."

"Merci. That will keep the ravenous wolves and their guests at bay tonight." Though Jean-Claude rarely had a kind word for the men he served three meals a day, Lilly knew most of it was in jest.

"Need I tell you what you often tell me, that your talents are wasted here?"

He waved away her compliment. "*Vous aussi?* Another voice to tickle my ears and tempt me to do something dangerous. If I open my own restaurant, it will become a success, of course, and that can only mean trouble."

"But that was so long ago. Surely no one remembers a handful of gems disappearing eleven years ago. The rich woman probably found her missing jewels soon after you left London. Isn't it likely everyone now knows you didn't take them, and you would be welcomed back to the Savoy with open arms? Not that I want you to leave this country. What about Chicago, or New York?"

"Alas, I could never leave my Mamie."

All she knew about Jean-Claude's lady friend was that she lived in another town and he visited her every Sunday. She was the reason he had come to Wisconsin. "Take her with you!"

A wistful look crossed his face. "Sadly, that would never happen."

"Well, I give up then, but a classically trained chef hiding out in the Northwoods is…" She fumbled for the right word. "It's blasphemy!"

Eyes wide, Jean-Claude stared at her. "How did you arrive at that?"

"God has gifted you with skills. No one, maybe no one in all of North America, can make chocolate mousse, *tarte flambée, hachis Parmentier,* or *soupe de poisson* like you." The French names rolled off her tongue, so much more elegant than flaming tart, meat pie, and fish stew. "And you are fixing these delicacies—these heavenly creations that bless one's palate with flavors found nowhere else—for a bunch of loud, brash, heathen louts. It is akin to casting pearls before swine!"

Jean-Claude held one hand to his forehead. "Oh, my dear, you have convicted me. You have pierced my heart with your effusive compliments." The slightest of smiles teased one corner of his handlebar moustache. "How can I possibly return to my old cookstove and sad little camp kitchen when greatness awaits?" He thrust out his arm...and came within inches of striking Bette in the face.

Bette huffed and took a step back. "*Mister* Pascal, kindly stop bothering the help."

As she whipped past him, Jean-Claude stuck out his tongue then smiled knowingly at Lilly. "Maybe," he whispered, "when I escape to New York City, I will take the famous butterfly pie girl with me. But, alas, I believe that would break the heart of a certain someone. Someone the size of a bull moose who could easily break me."

For the third time in minutes, a man winked at her. At least this wink she could decipher.

∽ CHAPTER TWO ∽

The Monday morning sun wouldn't show its face for two more hours, but the work that lay ahead forced Élan's feet out from under the quilt and onto the cold plank floor. His mind swirled with to-dos as he dressed and left the warmth of his cabin behind.

Several of the men he'd counted on returning in November hadn't, which meant that instead of making work schedules and overseeing the beginning of the logging season, he was stuck with inspecting equipment and repairing parts himself.

This morning, his main job was mending a broken runner on the ice sled. That would involve first jacking it up on blocks, a task he couldn't accomplish without help. He'd grab the first man he saw at breakfast and get on it. But breakfast was still an hour away.

He knocked bits of dry leaves and pine needles off his boots before entering the cook shanty. If the little Frenchman had his way, all the men would use the boot scraper he'd insisted Élan install next to the door. Giving in to Jean-Claude's whims out of fear of losing the best camp cook in all the northern states, Élan had sunk the metal bar in concrete three years ago. It had yet to be used.

The dining room, when it was empty and quiet, was one of his favorite places, second only to being alone in the small clearing surrounded by forty-foot pines half a mile from camp. The room reminded him of his father's church…when his father wasn't up front pounding the pulpit and the pews weren't filled with stuffy men in starched collars and women in flouncy dresses and too much perfume. How he'd loved to sneak into the sanctuary in the evening, carrying a single candle. He loved the sound of his footsteps echoing as he walked down the aisle to kneel at the altar. His father, always busy calling on his parishioners, never knew of this habit he had, never knew that, even though his only son had left the seminary after two years, his faith was strong and vibrant and more alive in the forest and in this log-walled room than it ever could have been in a fancy city church.

What would his men say if they knew their foreman prayed over this room every morning and walked around the camp at the close of every day, thanking God for safety and provision? He lifted his requests—for more men, for health and protection from injury, for good weather well into the season—then stepped into the kitchen.

Still dark. No sign of the little Frenchman who should be up by now, bustling about, giving commands to his minions. No fire blazed in the cookstove. With a frustrated sigh, Élan grabbed a handful of kindling. When he had a small fire going, he added several larger logs then picked up the blue-speckled enamel coffeepot and started making coffee. It wasn't that he was above the menial chore of coffee-making. It was just that he paid the arrogant chef well to keep the workers happy, and that included himself.

As he walked toward the door to the chef's quarters, his gaze landed on the lumpy forms of several pies covered in white floursack towels. He lifted the corner of one and gave another sigh as he looked at the golden-brown edges of the butterfly on top. This sigh was also of frustration.

"Papillon," he whispered.

Somewhere he'd heard someone describe butterflies as elusive. He could not agree more. His butterfly, the one he could only call his in his mind and dreams, was always just beyond his reach. So beautiful, so colorful and full of life and laughter. But not his. Never his.

A sliver of pie wouldn't do anything for his Lilly-generated frustration, but it might ease his irritation at the overpaid chef. He pulled a small metal plate from a shelf then reached for the handle of the forbidden drawer where Jean-Claude kept his collection of knives made in France. The knives had handles crafted from cow horn, and Jean-Claude demonstrated the razor sharpness of the blades to every new kitchen hire by holding up a sheet of paper and slicing through it as if it were made of butter. The demonstration was always followed by him pointing the blade at a trembling apprentice and the unfinished warning—"If you ever touch one of these..."

Élan tugged on the wooden handle. The drawer jerked open. Silently. No rattle of knives. He looked down. The drawer was empty. He turned around. No knives in the galvanized tub used to clear the tables.

The knives were gone.

Stifling a yawn, Lilly pulled four loaves of perfectly browned bread from the oven.

"Some of your best," Dottie called from her place in front of the other cookstove.

"You always say that."

"'Tis always true. I've watched your skills improving for nigh on six years now. Every day your baking gets prettier and prettier and tastier and tastier. I heard what that pipsqueak chef told you yesterday. You should take him up on his offer to fly this chicken coop. You could be working in one of those fancy kitchens with electric toasters and gas stoves and running water."

"You're talking to the wrong Galloway girl, Dot. I'd feel like I was suffocating in a place with so many people. I'd miss the smell of pine and the rush of the river. Give me the outdoors, a good woodstove, and enough lamp oil to read by at night, and I'll be happy forever."

Dottie wiped her hands on the once-white apron that stretched over her middle. "You know it warms my heart to hear that. I surely dunna want you to leave. You're the only thing standin' between me and gettin' fired by Miss Bette Be Ornery. I just hope you know your talents aren't being showcased like they should be here."

Lilly tipped a crusty loaf out of its pan then walked over to the woman who had filled a lot of the cracks in her soul after her parents died. Wrapping her arm around Dottie's shoulders, she said, "And you're all that's standing between me and losing my sanity."

"S'pose we need each other then." Dottie sniffed.

As she pulled away, Lilly looked down. There was a slight divot in the wood plank under Dottie, caused not just from her standing in front of the stove for hours on end, but from the shuffle-hop of her feet as she sang hymns with an Irish lilt to her voice and a spring in her step. When Bette criticized her for "having fun when you should be working," or tried to reprimand her with a withering look, Dottie was quick to quote Scripture in her defense. On any given day she might spout, "Thou hast turned for me my mourning into dancing,"

"Let them praise His name in the dance: let them sing praises unto Him with the timbrel and harp," or "And David danced before the LORD with all his might."

"We definitely need each—" A loud bang, ricocheting off the walls of the empty dining room, startled them both. "Was th-that a gunshot?" Lilly squeaked.

"Nay. 'Tis the front door bangin'."

Bette's shriek was the next sound to bounce off the walls.

Lilly ran to the kitchen door and flung it open. Élan stood two feet inside the foyer, his mud-caked boots making a mess on the floor. She could hear his heavy breathing from where she stood. As if he'd run the two miles from the camp. But the sight behind him proved he hadn't. His horse was tethered to the porch railing. Not to the hitching post, but right there in front, blocking the stairs. And it was not alone. A second saddled horse stood beside it, but no rider was in sight.

Her gaze whipped back to his face. His eyes were wild. She'd never before seen Élan Lamoreaux panic about anything. She stepped toward him. "What happened? Is someone hurt?"

Élan shook his head. "I don't...think so. Jean-Claude"—he stopped to catch his breath—"is gone."

"Gone?" Lilly pressed a hand to her chest. The look on Élan's face could only mean one thing. "He's...dead?"

"No! He's...gone. Just...gone. He left."

Without saying goodbye? She scrunched her eyes shut and took a deep breath. This was her fault. She'd been the one to suggest he belonged in Chicago or New York City. "I'm so sorry, Moose." Her eyes misted. How would she keep going without Jean-Claude's encouragement and teaching? "He will be hard to replace, won't he?"

"Hard?" Élan's voice boomed. "It will be impossible! The man is a culinary genius. Most of my men are here just because of his fancy cooking. I'm constantly fighting with Mr. Greeley about increasing their pay, but he stubbornly refuses. I'm shorthanded, and the men who have returned are here because of the food."

"Send them here," Bette offered. "We can feed them until you find a replacement."

"No. That's not a solution. Do you know what it would take to bring more than thirty men here three times a day?" His soulful gaze turned back to Lilly. "Papillon. You are my only hope."

Lilly's heart pounded, missing beats, and her legs began to lose their ability to hold her upright. She had no idea what he meant, but if he continued to look at her like that, she was in danger of agreeing to just about anything he would ask. "I…" Her mouth formed words, but no sound came out. She swallowed and tried again. "I have four loaves of bread I can send with you, and I'm sure Dottie can—"

"No. It will not be enough. Jean-Claude taught you. I know you prefer baking, but you can make anything he could. Papillon, please, come with me. If you don't, I will have a mutiny on my hands. The men will leave, the camp will close, the sawmill will shut down, and the town will die." He thrust his hand out to her. "You are the only one who can save Embarrass. We need you." Storm clouds brewed in his blue eyes. "*I* need you, my papillon."

Lilly gripped the back of a chair in each hand. Numbly, mesmerized by his gaze, feeling as if she no longer had control over her own reactions and merely stood in the wings watching, she nodded. "I'll get my coat."

∞ CHAPTER THREE ∞

"Over my dead body!" Bette stepped forward, hands on hips.

Lilly had seen some very unladylike anger from her sister, generally directed at the lumberjacks who spit tobacco into empty coffee cups or told off-color jokes when women and children were present. She'd even been the recipient of some of Bette's ire, but never had she seen this fire in her eyes.

"Under no circumstances will I allow my sister to go off into the woods to cook for a horde of uncivilized beasts with absolutely no respect for a lady. Mr. Lamoreaux, I am shocked you would even consider asking."

Élan stood like a statue, eyes wide in a face that appeared carved in stone. His lips parted. Lilly was about to speak for him when he said, "She will be well compensated, Miss Galloway. Jean-Claude has been receiving a salary far, far above the usual wage paid a camp cook. All of that will now go to Lilly for as long as we employ her. She'll have Sundays off, and I will commence finding a new cook immediately, but for—"

"No. Absolutely not. I will not permit it."

"He's not asking you. He's asking me. And I am going." Lilly was shocked by the calm and conviction in her own voice.

Bette's jaw unhinged. "You. Are. Not. What would Father say if he knew I allowed you to put yourself in such a compromising position? Mother would have a conniption."

"Mother and Father are gone. I am a legal adult, two weeks from my twenty-third birthday. I am capable of making my own decisions." Lilly folded her arms across her chest and jutted her chin forward. Not a mature pose. After announcing that she was an adult, she was now acting like a petulant child. She squared her shoulders, rising to her full height, which was, sadly, four inches shorter than her sister. "I will go with Élan. I will make breakfast for the men, prepare sandwiches for their dinner, and start a stew for supper, and then I will return in time to bake the biscuits for our dinner crowd and more bread for supper. You will hardly know I'm gone."

The stamp of her sister's foot resounded off the ceiling. Now who was acting like a child? "I. Will. Not. Allow it. When you arrived here, you came under my protection. You have been too sheltered. You're a naive girl, unfamiliar with the ways of the world. I will not allow you to put yourself in danger in a place where you would be the only woman and—"

Élan cleared his throat. "Evening Star is there. I can make sure she is in the kitchen with Papi—with Lilly at all times. I think she would be happy to help."

"Evening Star may be a woman, but she is not a—"

Lilly held her breath, praying Bette would not put words to her prejudice. Evening Star was a beautiful young Menominee, about Lilly's age, wedded to one of the lumberjacks who stayed year-round. Lilly had often accompanied her berry picking or foraging. Taking a walk with Evening Star was like attending a botany class in the forest. Lilly had learned to identify edible plants like lamb's quarters, prairie onion, wild leeks, wintergreen, and wild ginger, and often incorporated them in her baking. In return, Lilly had helped

Evening Star with her English. Since her husband, Slim, was a man of few words, she was always grateful for someone to talk to.

"There." Lilly interrupted before Bette could complete her unsavory comment. "It's settled. Evening Star and I work well together. I will enjoy her company." Turning to Élan and showing, or at least attempting to show, far more courage than she felt in the moment, she said, "Give me a couple of minutes to gather my things." With that, she turned on her heel and almost ran into the protective warmth of the kitchen. And Dottie's arms.

"'Twas a brave, brave thing ye did there, Lilly girl. It's proud of you I am, but worried too. You just be sure to stay close to Evening Star. They won't be botherin' you if you're with her, worried about her husband and all." She held out a cloth bag. "I took the liberty of packin' a few things for ya. I expect the little Frenchman took his best herbs and spices with him, so you'll be wantin' these if you're assigned the job of keepin' the men from wanderin' off to find a camp with a better cook."

Lilly looked in the bag, and her eyes misted. Along with a clean apron and Lilly's favorite paring knife and rolling pin, Dottie had given her at least half a dozen small parchment pouches, likely filled with herbs she'd grown and dried herself. "It smells heavenly."

"As will the camp kitchen when you're in it. Now get yer coat. Ya know that yer sister, she makes a lot of noise, but there ain't no storm behind that wind. She loves ya' and don't always know how to show it, ya ken?"

"I do. And I'm guilty of the same. Maybe not being in each other's way all the time will be good for us."

"Oh, yah, that it might. And maybe bein' in someone else's way will also be good for ya. Now off with ya.'" Dottie laughed and winked and gave Lilly a playful shove toward the coat hooks by the back door. When Lilly had her coat buttoned, Dottie pulled a sprig of holly from a jar that sat on the windowsill. "Take a bit o' brightness with ya." She wrapped it in a towel and placed it in the cloth bag. "Let it remind ya I'm prayin' for ya."

Lilly leaped into the saddle before Élan had a chance to assist her. No sidesaddle riding for her, much to her sister's horror. Though the door to the hotel had closed with a bang behind her, she had no doubt Bette was watching through the window and huffing like a steam engine.

Élan tied her cloth bag behind her saddle then patted the horse's neck. "This is Sweet Pea. She's gentle as a kitten and she's yours for as long as you have need of her. She'll have no trouble getting you to camp in the dark, but if you want, I can send a man to get you before dawn each day."

Lilly shook her head. "Sweet Pea and I will be fine."

He untied the reins. Before handing them over, he glanced up at her. It was the first time she'd ever seen him from this perspective. In the glow of a gas streetlamp, she looked down at the black hair that curled out around his beaver fur cap and the dark lashes that shaded those sky-blue eyes. Her heart did a little flutter, and she scolded herself. This was business. Nothing more. Élan needed her help. The entire town needed her help. Despite Bette's scoffing, there was absolute truth in what he'd said. If the men weren't happy, they would leave. If no logging started in the next few weeks, the sawmill would shut down and the men who worked there wouldn't have money to spend at the mercantile or for Sunday dinners at the hotel. Like the wooden blocks she'd set up in a line on the floor when she was a child, tipping one would make them all fall.

It was up to Lilly Galloway to save the town of Embarrass from disappearing off the map forever. With a deep breath and a prayer for confidence, she held out her hand for the reins.

"You cannot know how much this means to me, Papillon. Most ladies would never be so brave."

"I'm not so sure it is bravery. It may be boredom." She laughed at the look of confusion on his face then swept her arm out in front of her. "I thought when I came north to this rugged wilderness that life would be filled with adventure. Instead, it is filled with pies. Not that I don't love my job, but there's a whole world out here I long to explore."

Now it was his turn to laugh. "We shall have to see what we can do about that. Your adventure begins today. It is a man's job to rescue damsels in distress, no? But today you are the rescuer. You are my heroine, mademoiselle." He handed her the reins, tugged on the bill of his furry cap, and mounted his own horse.

They rode through town side by side. Two women, silhouetted by the light from the mercantile window, whispered behind gloved hands. Mrs. Tremblay and Mrs. Bernard, self-appointed spreaders of gossip, would make sure the whole town knew that Lilly Galloway and Élan Lamoreaux had brazenly ridden together right down the middle of Main Street. She felt a twinge of remorse for what the rumors and speculations would do to Bette. It was sure to damage her standing in the social order of the little backwoods town of less than three hundred backwoods souls.

The twinge of guilt dissipated as the street turned into a two-rut wagon path and the woods closed in around them. She loved the muffled sound of horse hooves on pine needles. With each bend in the path, she felt the tense muscles in her shoulders relaxing.

And then Élan smiled at her.

Involuntarily, her arm, the one with the hand attached that held the reins, jerked back. Sweet Pea's head reared, and the horse whinnied as she came to a sudden stop. Élan whirled around to Lilly, his gaze scanning the woods and then the ground. "What spooked her?"

You. Or rather you spooked me. But she couldn't say that. "I… uh…thought I saw something." Something in those clear blue eyes that ought to have a lake named after them. "Sorry."

"Not to worry. We're almost there. Are you finding her easy to handle?"

Much easier than you. "Yes. She lives up to her name. Who named her?"

In the dim dawn light, she could see a slight tinge of pink on those bewhiskered cheeks again. "I did."

Lilly turned to gaze at the spring-fed stream they were passing. Anything to hide the smile she couldn't restrain. "It fits her. What do you call yours?"

The pink darkened. "Lollipop."

Lollipop and Sweet Pea? Lilly couldn't have held back a grin if someone had offered her all the tea in China.

He squinted at her. "I happen to know you named your rolling pin."

She supposed it should be her turn to blush, but she felt no embarrassment. "I was only following Jean-Claude's orders. He says a proficient pastry chef must fall in love with the tools of her trade. How can you fall in love with an unnamed object?"

The tanned skin around Élan's eyes crinkled into lines that reminded her of sunrays. She was sure he would burst out laughing at her, but instead he merely blushed a bit fiercer. "But…F-fanny?" he stuttered.

Oh my. Heat crept up her neck. What was he thinking? "Fannie *Farmer.* I named her for Fannie Farmer."

Clearly, the name did not ring a bell. The poor man looked more confused than ever.

"She wrote a cookbook. *The Boston Cooking-School Cook Book.* I saved my money for a whole year so I could order it. Fannie introduced the idea of standardized measuring spoons and cups. Not that I stick to those now that I've learned to be more intuitive the way Jean-Claude taught me, but I so love her…" She clamped her lips shut. "Bette is always chastening me about blathering."

"Not at all. Your sister is wrong about that. There is a misconception among women that men do not like women who talk too much. In truth, most of us are fascinated by those who, like you, have something to say. It is the women, and men for that matter, who have nothing to say but continue to blather that try anyone's patience."

"You are too kind."

"I am not a flatterer, Papillon. I will never give anyone a compliment I do not mean. Returning to your statement about unnamed objects, I have a similar philosophy, only I believe it is the reverse. Every axe I have ever owned is named Jenny."

"Why?"

"Because how can an object love you if you have not given it a name?"

Their laughter blended as smooth and sweet as butter and confectioners' sugar. "How thoughtless of me not to be aware of my rolling pin's affection for me."

"Well, from now on you will feel more appreciated, yes?" His eyes told her he meant more than what his teasing words said.

"Yes." In truth, she had never felt more appreciated than she did at that very moment.

Élan gestured to a clearing. "We'll hitch the horses by my cabin."

Lilly slid off Sweet Pea and tied her reins to the post next to the cabin's front step. She'd been to the camp many times, delivering pies or taking lessons from Jean-Claude, but she'd never ventured beyond the cook shanty. She'd never gotten a close look at the little log house Élan called home. Gingham curtains hung in its two windows. Who had made them? What was it like inside? Was it cozy, with a rocking chair on a braided rug in front of the hearth and a colorful quilt on the bed, or stark and utilitarian, simply a place for the bachelor boss to kick off his boots and sleep?

As they neared the cook shanty, she became aware of a muffled noise, almost like a distant swarm of bees or the low rumble of an approaching train still a couple of miles away. "What is that sound?"

Élan grinned. "That…is the sound of insurrection. A sound that is about to come to a halt." He stepped in front of her and put his hand on the doorknob. The heavy door creaked as he opened it. A cacophony resounded from within. From behind Élan, she got a glimpse of six long tables filled with men, all making noise at once.

Grumbling, swearing, singing, laughing. Discordant and foreign to her ears, it reminded Lilly of an orchestra tuning up. A slice of bread whizzed past the opening just as Élan stepped into the room.

The commotion came to an instant halt. In seconds, the only sounds were the smacking of boots on wood and the scrape of benches. And then complete silence.

"Good morning, men." Élan spoke with an exaggerated warmth that confused Lilly. "I do hope you've enjoyed your few minutes of frivolity as much as I will enjoy docking an hour of your wages."

"Where's Jean-Claude?" one of them shouted. "It's past six. Those lunkheads in the kitchen don't know beans about—"

"Jean-Claude is gone. Breakfast is underway. Anyone wishing to wait, in silence, can start work late."

He made a sharp pivot, the way she would imagine a palace guard turning, and took a step toward the kitchen, no longer shielding her from the men.

"Butterfly girl!" one of the men in back whispered. "We'll be eatin' good with—"

Élan squelched his words with a look then held the kitchen door open for her. As the door closed behind him, not a sound could be heard from the men.

"How did you do that?"

"Silence is the rule in the dining room. They are only allowed to speak if they need something from a server. But, how does the saying go…when the cat's away…"

"Or, in this case, the moose." She flashed him a smile and turned to greet the men who'd started cooking breakfast. "Good morning, Tobias, Hen—" Her words caught in her throat. "Auguste!"

Jean-Claude's prize rolling pin, marked with the seal of the famous French chef who trained him, sat on a shelf next to the window, its place of honor. Lilly pressed her hand to her chest. "He would never, ever, have willingly left Auguste." Fear coursing through her, she turned to Élan. "Something is very, very wrong."

❧ Chapter Four ❧

The smell of cooking apples and the sound of something frying assured Lilly that she would have a little help in her quest to save the town.

Tobias Mueller, Jean-Claude's assistant cook, looked up from presiding over two massive cast-iron frying pans and glared at her. She'd always felt Tobias viewed her as his competition. For what, she wasn't sure. For Jean-Claude's attention? Possibly. And now, here she was taking over what he likely thought would be his kitchen in Jean-Claude's absence. Diplomacy would be needed.

"Sure am glad you're here, Mr. Lamoreaux," George said, setting a tray on the table. "We tried gettin' 'em to be quiet, but they weren't havin' it. Nice to see you too, ma'am." He nodded at Lilly then turned back to Élan. "So where is Jean-Claude? We couldn't make sense outa what you said when you woke us up."

"Thought I was dreaming for a bit," Henry said, "when all you did was yell to wake us up. Way better than Jean-Claude singing that awful song about taking his baby to a party."

Lilly furrowed her brow at Henry then looked at Élan, who leaned against a cabinet, hands in his pockets. He turned away from her, but not before she saw his smile. "*Enfant*," he said. "Not baby." The effort not to burst out laughing caused a vein at his temple to bulge. And then, to her shock, he began to sing. "*Allons enfants de la Patrie. Le jour de gloire est arrivé...*" His rich, deep voice filled the kitchen. She was aware she was gaping at him, but she couldn't seem to figure out how to close her mouth.

"'La Marseillaise,'" he explained. "The national anthem of France. It means something like, 'Let's go, child of the fatherland. The day of glory has arrived.'"

"It's…intriguing." More the singer than the song, but she couldn't let him know that. "Very majestic."

"So where *is* Jean-Claude?" George repeated.

"Gone," Tobias answered. "Not here. Absent."

"Wasn't asking you," George said, and received a seething look from Tobias.

"So…" Lilly slipped out of her coat as she stepped closer. "What's on the menu, Tobias?"

"Regular food." He turned from the stove, pulled a piece of paper from his pocket, and shoved it across the table in her direction.

Today's breakfast menu was written on the paper in Jean-Claude's tight, slanted handwriting. In French. Next to each line, in bold, vertical penmanship that seemed to her defiant, Tobias had written the translation. Not just in English but, more specifically, in lumberjack language.

She covered the right side with one hand and read through the menu as Jean-Claude had written it. She'd learned enough French to know that Tobias had butchered it, probably deliberately.

Crêpes aux pommes compotes
Omelette soufflée aux champignons et poivrons
Côte de porc frite avec graines de fenouil et pommes de terre rôties
La tarte de Lilly

She translated the first line. Crepes with stewed apples. Tobias had written "flapjacks and apples." In Tobias's translation, the soufflé omelet with mushrooms and peppers had become "scrambled eggs," and fried side pork with fennel seed and roasted potatoes was reduced to "bacon and potatoes." The last line widened her smile. La tarte de Lilly. Lilly's pie.

"Looks like you have things well under control," she said. "What can I do?"

Tobias appeared surprised by her question. Did he really think she'd just barge in and start barking orders?

"Flapjack batter's all ready, and the griddle's heated." He nodded to the cookstove.

"I'll get started on that then." As she pulled her apron out of the cloth bag Dottie had packed for her, a paper-wrapped bundle fell out. She picked it up and sniffed it. Fennel.

Élan's words came back to her. *The man is a culinary genius. Most of my men are here just because of his fancy cooking. I'm short-handed, and the men who have returned are here because of the food.*

Tying the apron with a strong, decisive knot, she took a deep breath and set about doing what her moose had hired her to do.

Élan watched, hands fisted. This was not what he'd wanted. He'd hoped Lilly would march in and take over Jean-Claude's role, handing each person their orders and not giving an inch.

He'd wanted her to be whatever the feminine version of the little Frenchman looked like, but within the first five minutes Tobias had taken the upper hand, setting the tone for what was sure to be a disaster. Of course, today was an exception, but he hoped she knew that tomorrow had to be different. Realizing that some of the blame probably rested with him, he stepped closer to Lilly, ready to say, "We have a reputation to uphold. We get by on paying these men minimum wages because they stay for the food. If we're going to feed them the same fare they can get at any..."

The conversation he was rehearsing faded. Something was happening.

Lilly opened a paper packet about the size of her hand then picked up what looked like a bundle of weeds. "Tobias, the menu called for fennel in the pork. Do you know if the men like it?"

"They love it. They asked what made the side pork taste so good last time we served it."

"Wonderful." She set the bundle on the stove next to him then stepped over to the sideboard and pulled two large tins from the cupboard and handed them to George, who'd begun cracking eggs into a bowl. "How about mushrooms and peppers to add a little color?" she suggested. "I know Tobias and Jean-Claude spent a lot of time drying them."

Henry looked up. "I'll add some cinnamon to the apples, and a tiny bit of cayenne pepper. Did you know, Miss Lilly, that a little heat can bring out the sweetness?"

Lilly smiled. "I think I'm going to learn a lot from you three." She returned to the crock and added a few pinches of something reddish brown to the batter. Nutmeg. Élan could smell it from where he stood.

As the first batch of fragrant flapjacks cooked, Lilly reached into her cloth bag and brought out something wrapped in a small white towel. She unwrapped it carefully. He recognized it as winterberry. Bright red orbs against shiny green leaves. She twisted the towel into a tight circle, secured the end, and then wedged the winterberry upright in the center. A miniature Christmas tree.

"Uh-oh." Henry laughed and pointed. The other two men turned, shook their heads, and then began laughing too.

"What? It's not that silly." Lilly's chin jutted.

"If Jean-Claude were here, he would pitch that thing as far as he could," Tobias said.

"Zese colors are not allowed in ze kitchen!" George's accent perfectly captured Jean-Claude's inflection. "His archrival at the Savoy, a man from Venice, wore a silk scarf that was a replica of the flag of Italy every day just to irritate the French chefs."

"But Jean-Claude had the last laugh," Tobias added. "He was awarded the coveted rolling pin the other guy thought he would get."

"I never heard that." Lilly touched a red berry with her fingertip. "But Jean-Claude is not here, so my little tree stays." She held up one finger. "Zis is our kitchen for now."

The men laughed again and turned back to their work. Élan's shoulders dropped, and his chest expanded with his first full breath since the moment he'd walked into a kitchen that didn't smell like coffee.

Everything would be fine. The men were in good hands. Soft, pretty, petite, but oh, so competent hands. After another relieved exhale, he said, "I'll go find Evening Star."

"Wait." Emerald eyes pierced him, and then she turned and began ladling circles of batter onto the griddle. Over her shoulder she asked, "What are you going to do about Jean-Claude?"

"Do?"

"To find him."

He rubbed the back of his neck. "I'm not so sure he wants to be found. I'm guessing he's off in search of a better job."

The ladle clanked against the crock. "He would not have left without Auguste."

"Maybe he just forgot it." Élan stood with his thumbs hooked in his pockets, not knowing what to do as Lilly, face reddening, picked up the rolling pin and held it out to him as if it were a smoking gun.

"Never. Don't you understand?" She placed the rolling pin gently back on its shelf. "This is his most prized possession in all the world. Auguste is a symbol of what he could have become. It represents everything that was wonderful about his life before he was wrongly accused of stealing from that duchess. It was a gift from Georges-Auguste Escoffier, the world-renowned pastry chef who believed Jean-Claude Pascal would someday take on his mantle, becoming the next great chef to impact the culinary world."

"You believe all that?"

Lilly appeared to freeze. The normally soft contours of her face seemed suddenly chiseled in granite. For a moment, he was afraid she was going to throw the ladle, or maybe the whole crock, at him. "Why wouldn't I believe it?"

"Well…" How to explain without making her even angrier? "He's a…short man…living with lumberjacks. He makes doughnuts. We chop down forty-foot trees."

"What is your point?"

Élan cleared his throat. "We all…tell stories. Tall tales. We make our exploits seem bigger, more…stupendous than they really are."

"You're saying you think he lied about being trained by Chef Escoffier?"

"Maybe not lied. Exactly. Maybe he stretched the truth."

"Posh," Lilly sputtered. "Nonsense. He has a signed certificate. How many lumberjacks eat croissants and peach melba? And you've seen the cookbook he wrote."

"If he is, in fact, Jean-Claude Pascal."

Her eyes bored into him. It reminded him of when he was a boy, using his father's magnifying glass to burn holes in leaves. And, though he never told his father, and felt terrible about it now, to roast ants. At the moment, he felt like one of those roasting ants.

He didn't want to tell Lilly what he really thought about Jean-Claude's stories. The first time he'd set eyes on the man, he'd looked like a drowned rat, just off the boat in Green Bay. In the hour Pascal had stood on the dock asking for work, someone had stolen one of his bags. He was penniless and hungry.

Élan had been hoping to hire immigrants looking for work. Big, strong men, hopefully with some experience in logging or farming or construction. He'd found four of those, and one who looked like he'd struggle to wield a three-pound axe. But the man who stood eye-to-chest with him had claimed he could cook food "that will make you think you have died and gone to the great beyond." So, Élan had brought him back to camp, threatening to fire him if his cooking didn't live up to his claim. It had only taken one meal—salmon with hollandaise, roasted potatoes, fresh green beans with slivered almonds, followed by peach melba with whipped cream—to convince him the demanding Frenchman could stay.

To this day, Élan had no idea where the man had acquired almonds. Nor did he know if any of his story of being wrongly accused of theft was real.

"Did he take a horse?" Lilly asked.

In his hurry this morning, that thought had never occurred to him. With Lilly's gaze nailing him against the cupboard, he felt foolish. He knew the answer to that question. As he'd searched for just the right horse for Lilly, he'd walked past every stall in the shed, past the draft horses and those reserved for riding. Sweet Pea was at the end. Every other stall was occupied. "No," he said sheepishly. "He didn't."

"Then that is proof. He did not leave of his own accord."

Jean-Claude had been abducted. It was the only explanation. Lilly could see it play out in her mind. In the middle of the dark and moonless night, someone had snuck into his room and knocked him over the head, carrying him off. Maybe he'd just lost consciousness. Maybe he was dead. The thought made her heart stop and then thud against her ribs.

Who had taken him? And why? Only one thing made sense. The people who had falsely accused him of stealing jewels from a duchess in London had come to America and hunted him down. Unless...

She knew this kitchen as well as the Galloways'. This was where, when she was sixteen, Jean-Claude had taught her the meaning of terms like amandine, ragout, beurre blanc, hollandaise, soufflé, demi-glace, and escalope. On the massive worktable in the center of the room she had learned the *fraisage* method of making piecrust by using the heel of her hand to smear the butter into the flour, a technique Bette had yelled at her for until she tasted the light, flaky result.

This was where she'd learned to use knives that cut through tomatoes as if they were made of whipping cream, and crimpers, wooden paddles, cookie stamps, and whisks. She turned and yanked open a drawer.

All of Jean-Claude's precious tools were gone. All but Auguste. Why? Surely not an oversight. Even if he had been in a hurry, the rolling pin would be the first thing he would pack.

Leaving Auguste behind was a sign. A secret message. A cry for help.

✑ CHAPTER FIVE ✑

The dining room was empty. The tables were cleared. Water for washing dishes was heating on the stove. Bread dough was rising. Lilly leaned against the doorframe and soaked in the silence of the camp dining room. The crackle of the fire in the massive iron stove and the squawk of a blue jay outside the wavy-glass nine-pane windows were the only sounds.

This room felt like a church when it was empty. What was it like here when an itinerant preacher came to camp? Was attendance at services mandatory, like silence at meals? Or did only a handful show up? It was likely a preacher would feel he wasted his time and breath on men who prided themselves on being coarse, crude, and independent.

She startled when the door opened. Evening Star stood in the doorway, surrounded by a halo of sunlight. Lilly ran to her. It had been almost a month since they'd last met to gather mushrooms in the woods. They embraced, and Evening Star said, "I am so sorry I could not come right away. I was not feeling well."

Lilly stepped back. "Are you all right now?" Then she noticed something different. Evening Star's face seemed rounder. She appeared tired, and yet her eyes shimmered with their usual joy. Evening Star's hands rested on her belly.

She didn't ask, but she didn't need to.

Evening Star nodded. "When the last snow melts."

"I'm so happy for you." And then, staring at her friend's protective hand on her middle, another reality settled in her chest. Not only was she charged with the job of saving the camp to save the mill to save the town, now that charge bore a face. A tiny, yet-to-be-born face. She squared her shoulders. "Are you sure it won't bother you to cook?"

"I am fine now, though I may be of little help in the mornings for a while."

"We will survive without you. Come." Lilly opened the door to the kitchen. "I'll have bread baking in an hour, and Jean-Claude had a pot of beans soaking. I'm sure he intended to do something very French with them, but he only had a menu made out for breakfast, so I put them on to cook with some side pork and molasses for dinner."

"Flaggins."

"What?"

"It is what the men call the noonday meal."

"Well, I've never heard the word, but if that's what they call it then so be it. Flaggins it is. Our next task is to start cutting up meat and vegetables for supper. They do call it supper, don't they?"

Evening Star giggled. "Yes."

"The men are out back butchering. If you would like to start chopping carrots and potatoes, I'm going to hunt for Jean-Claude's cookbook." She stood on a chair and began searching the upper shelves, to no avail. "I should have brought the one he gave me. I need to find something to do with venison and vegetables that suits Mr. Lamoreaux's exotic palate."

"Ex-otic?"

"Oh, sorry. It is not a common word. It means something from another country, usually something fancy or special."

37

"Ah." Mischief danced in Evening Star's large brown eyes. "I think you are all the fancy and special Mr. Lamoreaux requires."

Heat blazed upward from under Lilly's starched white collar. She hopped down from the chair. "I'll…go look in his quarters." She rushed out of the kitchen and into Jean-Claude's room. She wondered how Evening Star knew. Was it that obvious? When had Evening Star seen her with Élan? Did she talk about him too much? Or…was it something *he* said? Evening Star's comment had implied something about Élan's thoughts of her. Hadn't it?

Jean-Claude's sparse little room was much cooler than the kitchen, giving her face time to return to its normal temperature. She took a moment to look around, hoping for some kind of clue as to why Jean-Claude had left. A threadbare quilt covered a cot. A dirty apron hung on a hook. No other clothes in sight. Two books sat next to a kerosene lamp on a small table. She picked them up, hoping they were French cookbooks. She was surprised at the top one. *La Sainte Bible.* She hadn't pictured Jean-Claude as a Bible-reading man. The second book was, indeed, a cookbook.

She ran her finger down the table of contents page until she found the word she was looking for. *Ragouts.* Stews. How easy it would be to make a simple venison stew with carrots and potatoes thickened with a bit of flour. *But I can be—I can do exotic if that is what Monsieur Lamoreaux requires.* She found a recipe for *blanquette de veau*, veal stew. There was no veal to be found here, but the doe she had seen on the table in back was not large. The meat would be tender. She didn't know the French word for venison, so tonight's menu would feature *blanquette de venison.*

She looked at the list of ingredients, skipping over the things they didn't have and calculating measurements for each item. Cayenne pepper, chives, parsley, thyme, bay leaves, coriander, carrots, onions, cream, butter, flour. She would add diced potatoes for substance. There would be no celery root or leeks or fresh lemon juice, but it was likely only one of the men they cooked for knew what blanquette de veau was supposed to taste like. Now all she had to do before heading back to the hotel was oversee the cubing of twenty pounds of raw meat.

Lilly wrinkled her nose at the thought. *This* was why she had chosen to bake pies and bread and leave to Dottie the processing of things that once walked the earth.

Keeping her finger in the page, she closed the book and clutched it to her chest. She had often heard that the way to a man's heart was through his stomach. This book she held in her hands just might be the key to unlocking a certain blue-eyed someone's stony heart.

As she turned to walk out of the room, an envelope fluttered out of the book and landed on the cot. She set the book down, picked up the envelope, and ran her finger across the embossed lettering of the address in the top left corner.

Palmer House Hotel
17 East Monroe Street
Chicago, Illinois

The letter was addressed to JCP at a post office box in Shawano, about twelve miles northwest. JCP, not his name. It reminded Lilly of monogrammed bath towels.

Was it an invasion of privacy to look inside the envelope? It had already been opened, and he had left it behind. After a moment of hesitation, she pulled out a single sheet of paper.

September 21, 1901
Dearest Jean-Claude,

I must say I was surprised and delighted to hear from you. I have oft wondered what became of you after you left the Savoy. Imagine my shock to discover you are here in the States, living in obscurity. This news grieves me, my friend.

I will get right to the point. Of course, I would be thrilled to have you working with me, but two things prevent me from offering the position. One is a fear for your safety. The other is concern for the reputation of the Palmer House. It is likely you are unaware of the yet well-kept secret of why Cesar Ritz and your mentor, Auguste Escoffier, were dismissed from the Savoy. In fact, I suppose it is possible you have no knowledge of their partnership, since you left before it began. Only a few of us on the inside know the details, but I shall share them with you, relying on your discretion to keep this quiet.

Four years ago, Ritz and Escoffier were implicated in the disappearance of large amounts of wines and spirits and for accepting gifts from the Savoy's suppliers. It is estimated they may have defrauded the Savoy of up to three million dollars! Because of the charges falsely pressed against you, and because your name is inextricably connected with Escoffier's, you can understand my reticence. However, if you were to

consider using an alias and writing yourself, as it were, a new
biography, I believe we could come to a mutual agreement.
I look forward to your response.

Sincerely,
Chef Joseph Seyl

Lilly looked again at the date the letter was written. Her encouragement may have been the straw that broke the camel's back, but if Jean-Claude left willingly to pursue this job, that decision was not on her shoulders. He had likely been planning to leave all along.

Still…why had he left Auguste?

Picking up the book, she turned and marched into the kitchen. There was nothing she could do about all of that now.

Now, she must cut vegetables and meat and make blanquette de venison and save the town. And the future of Evening Star's child.

CHAPTER SIX

On Tuesday morning, the temperature dropped below freezing for the first time. There was a buzz in camp, a kind of energy that was almost palpable. The men were getting restless, tired of hanging around patching clothing and fixing harnesses. They were anxious to head into the woods.

Élan remembered that feeling. His first few winters as a sawyer he'd been like a jittery horse, chomping at the bit to get out and start sawing. Now, after nine years, the last three in charge of hiring and scheduling and keeping a bunch of bullheaded men in line, he was starting to lose the thrill of the first cut. After he put on his coat and gloves, he walked out into a frost-coated world then turned and cast a longing look at his chair by the fire where his reading glasses sat atop his Bible.

He stepped into the cook shanty as George and Henry brought plates and bowls to the table. The smell of freshly-made doughnuts almost overshadowed the odor of forty unwashed men crammed in a room with no ventilation. He nodded at the men sitting quietly though looking impatient with forks and knives in hand, and stepped into the kitchen. The table was covered with cooling dough-nuts and massive cookies sparkling with sugar. Lilly stood, hands on hips, complimenting Tobias on wiping the edges of a platter of sausage garnished with flakes of something green. Tobias grinned when she said, "On mange d'abord avec les yeux." *We eat with our eyes first.*

"I used to hate those words," Tobias replied. "Every. Single. Day. Every time he said it, I pictured that cranky little Frenchman's eyes munching on flapjacks." When Lilly laughed, he added, "But you make it sound very nice, Miss Lilly."

Élan's fingers curled into his palms. This man, barely old enough to require a razor, was flirting with his Lilly. But, he reminded himself, that might be preferable to having him resistant to her every suggestion. He cleared his throat. "Everything going well?" He looked around. "Where is Evening Star?"

"She will…be here in a bit. We have made out a schedule. Her help isn't needed at breakfast. We'll work on din-flaggins together and start supper, then I will head back to the hotel and she'll take over from there."

There was something strange about her answer. She seemed embarrassed. Why? He'd had so little experience with women. The Bible commanded men to love and protect them, but he'd never read anything about understanding their ways.

"I'll fix you a plate." She smiled at him, and he dropped onto a stool at the end of the worktable. He'd once won a log-throwing contest, tossing a twenty-foot pole that weighed a hundred and seventy-five pounds farther than any competitors. Though his sawyer days were in the past, he could still, given the right partner, fell a four-foot-diameter white pine with a crosscut saw faster than any of the young bucks who worked for him. And yet, here he was, felled by a single smile.

Three hundred and thirty-seven days ago he'd made a promise to Lilly's sister, but it was a promise with an end date. And that date was coming up in twenty-eight days. If Bette couldn't find a buyer for the hotel by the end of the year, he was free to make his feelings known.

Lilly brought him a cup of coffee and a plate piled high with two doughnuts covered in sugar, five pieces of sausage, and an omelet filled with cheese and mushrooms. To his surprise, she dished up a plate for herself and sat across from him. "I have something to show you," she said in a conspiratorial whisper. She pulled an envelope from her apron pocket. "I found this in one of Jean-Claude's cookbooks."

His stomach growled as he took it, in agreement with his head that her timing was poor. But he read the letter then handed it back to her and sank his teeth into a warm, sugary doughnut, crispy on the outside and soft as a cloud on the inside. He chewed and swallowed. "Delicious. So, it appears he was not abducted in the middle of the night." He couldn't stop the smile that might infuriate her.

"This proves nothing. If he had accepted this job, he would not have left Auguste behind."

He tried to tame his expression. She spoke about the rolling pin as if it were a pet dog or maybe even a child. "According to the letter, the man he practically worshiped was a thieving scoundrel. Maybe, after learning that, he wanted nothing to do with the item you say represented his old life."

Lilly took a bite of egg and nodded slowly. "As much as I hate to admit it, it is possible you are right. I can't imagine how he must have felt when he learned that his esteemed mentor was guilty of the same thing he was falsely accused of doing." Her eyes widened. "Maybe it was Escoffier who took the jewels, and he let Jean-Claude take the fall for it. If Jean-Claude hadn't escaped…" She sipped her coffee and continued to nod.

"What was that you said a moment ago? You hate to admit it, but what?"

Her face broke into the most dazzling smile he'd seen yet. "You heard me, Monsieur Moose. I do not need to repeat myself."

"But you—"

The swinging door at the end of the kitchen flew open. George stood with an empty platter in each hand, his face white as a sheet. "M-Mr. Greeley is here. He wants a tour. He w-wants you to give a tour. There's someone w-with him."

Solomon Greeley, owner of the Soleil Rouge camp, usually wrote before coming out, but his appearance wasn't unusual enough to warrant George looking like he'd seen a ghost. "What's wrong? Who is with him?"

"M-Mister William Pinkerton, sir."

For the third time in three days, Lilly saw fear on the face of the man she'd once thought impervious to anxious thoughts. Élan paled at the mention of William Pinkerton. Was he one of *the* Pinkertons? From the Pinkerton Detective Agency? If so, why did that strike terror in George and Élan?

There could be only one reason. Guilt.

Élan stood, looking like he might topple over if a stiff wind blew through the door. He nodded woodenly. "I will…" His gaze swept the room, resting on her for just a moment. He appeared to be searching.

"Can I help you find something?" she asked.

"My coat."

Not wanting to embarrass him in front of George, she slid her hand across the table and touched her fingertip to the button on his sleeve. The sleeve of his coat.

"Oh. Yes. Right. I'll"—he glanced down at his half-eaten breakfast—"finish this later." With that, he turned and walked out of the kitchen.

Lilly looked at George, still standing like a statue with a platter in each hand. "What was that all about?"

"I dunno, ma'am. Mr. Greeley didn't seem pleased." His eyes shifted from the stove, where more sausage awaited the platters he held, to the door that led to the bunk room he and Henry and Tobias shared. And to Jean-Claude's room.

Did this have something to do with Jean-Claude? Though she wanted, with all her heart, to believe he was innocent and his tale of being wrongly accused was true, she had no way of knowing for sure.

Then again, this might be about Jean-Claude's disappearance. Maybe someone had reported it to Mr. Greeley. Maybe someone here in camp knew what had really happened to him.

What if the letter wasn't real but had been planted there by someone who had kidnapped Jean-Claude to turn him in? Years ago, when Jean-Claude first told her why he'd come to America, he'd said there was a bounty on his head. How much was it? Enough to cause someone to sail across the Atlantic in search of him? Maybe he'd tipped his hand when he wrote to the Palmer Hotel. The chef who answered his letter might not be his friend after all. He might be wanting to lure Jean-Claude to Chicago so he could claim the bounty.

Chicago. The Pinkerton Detective Agency was based there.

Henry walked in, a coffeepot in each hand. "Who was that with Greeley?" He aimed his question at George's back.

"William Pinkerton." George didn't turn around, but Lilly didn't miss the quick look he shot Henry. To silence him? "They're probably friends. You know how Greeley likes to show off his property." His voice was thick with disdain.

A chill slithered up Lilly's spine. What was going on here? The Pinkerton Agency handled big cases. Lilly had read every word printed in the *Clintonville Tribune* and the *Post Crescent* about the kidnapping in Omaha last Christmas. A fifteen-year-old boy, Eddie Cudahy, son of the millionaire owner of the Omaha Stockyards, was walking home when a carriage pulled up and a man jumped out and grabbed him. His father returned home late that night and discovered him missing. The next day, he closed the packing plant and asked his two thousand workers to hunt for his son.

Before long seven thousand people were out searching. Then the father received a phone call telling him to search his front yard. They found a ransom note demanding $25,000 for the boy's safe return. It instructed the father to go alone and leave the money, all in gold pieces, at a spot on the side of the road where he would find a lantern. The kidnappers warned that if he did not follow through, they would bring harm to his son.

Lilly shuddered. Had Mr. Greeley received a ransom note for the return of Jean-Claude? The Cudahy boy had returned home the next day, unharmed. Would their story turn out as well?

The incident in Nebraska had created a huge public outcry because the father had "given in" and paid the ransom. They blamed him for the kidnapper still being on the lam. Mr. Cudahy offered a reward for the capture of the kidnappers, and the kidnappers retaliated with threats, ordering him to retract the reward offer.

Lilly still remembered the poorly spelled and punctuated letter the *Crescent* had published, word for word. It contained statements like, "If any many whether gilty or innocent is ever arrested we will close the Boys mouth with A Bulet." It had ended with "You will think of this warning when it is too late."

Would Mr. Greeley refuse to pay a ransom demand if they received one? What was Jean-Claude to him? Nothing but an employee. Not a family member, not someone he cared about personally. Would William Pinkerton advise him not to pay? What evidence did they have to go on?

The letter! And Auguste! Lilly stood, toppling her stool, and picked up the letter. Then she grabbed the rolling pin from its place of honor on the wall beside the stove.

Poor Jean-Claude could be, right now, barely alive, maybe being tortured to confess a crime of which he was not guilty. And she held in her hand what might be the only evidence available to solve this case and rescue the poor man. Without bothering to put on her coat, she ran outside and yelled for Moose.

∽ Chapter Seven ∾

"Our two filers have been with the camp since the seventies. They both started out as sawyers, so they know the importance of a sharp saw. Of course, when they were young, all the felling was done with axes. Crosscut saws have only been used for the past ten—"

"Moose!"

Standing in the doorway of the filer's shanty, Élan stopped mid-sentence and grimaced at the two men he'd been speaking to then whirled around, his pulse halted by Lilly's cry. It took him only a second to spot her...running across the grass waving a rolling pin.

"What in the world?" He sprinted toward her, possibilities filling his mind like mud oozing over wagon wheels. Fire? A fight in the dining room? He mentally calculated the time it would take him to run to the wanigan—a mobile structure on wheels—and grab his medical supplies and get back to the cook shanty before someone bled to death. "What happened?" he yelled as he neared her.

She stopped a yard in front of him and bent over, catching her breath. "The l-letter. Give them the letter. And this." She thrust out the letter from the Palmer House Hotel in one hand and Jean-Claude's Auguste in the other.

"Whoa." Reaching over her outstretched hands, he clamped her upper arms, trying to calm and steady her the way he would Lollipop. "Slow down. Easy now. Give who what?"

"These are evidence. For the investigation."

"What investigation?" His thoughts followed the same track they'd dug just minutes ago. How did God expect a man to love and protect a woman when he had no idea what she was talking about?

She gaped at him as if he had, indeed, sprouted moose antlers. *Moose.* She'd called him Moose in front of his boss. And William Pinkerton. "To find Jean-Claude!" Her gaze shifted to over his shoulder. It was then he heard soft steps in the frosted grass behind him.

"Everything all right, Mr. Lamoreaux?" Mr. Greeley asked. "Miss...?"

Élan turned around. "This is Lilly Galloway, sir. Sirs. Our cook has taken a position elsewhere, and she is filling in."

"Ah." Mr. Greeley doffed his top hat. "The pie lady. I've heard much about you. In fact, I've heard jesting from a couple of other camp owners about kidnapping you for your pies." His laughter reverberated in the clearing.

"Kidnapping." Lilly swiveled to face Mr. Pinkerton.

Élan had no idea what she was about to say, but whatever it was, she was very likely about to make a laughingstock out of herself.

"That's what I came out here to tell you. Mr. Pinkerton, I have information to aid in your investigation."

Mr. Pinkerton shot a look at Élan that felt like daggers. Did he really think Élan could have revealed anything about the man's reason for being there? He hadn't been out of Pinkerton's sight since he'd been told about it. "What do you know about this case?"

"I know you're searching for the camp chef who was taken against his will sometime during the night on Sunday. We know he was taken against his will because he left this behind." She shoved the rolling pin at his chest.

Élan looked down at his feet and considered turning and running into the forest and never coming back. What could he do to rescue her? "Lilly, Mr. Pinkerton and Mr. Greeley served together during the war. Mr. Pinkerton and his family are visiting friends in Wausau, and he stopped by to get a tour of our operation." No need to tell her the two men had served together in the secret service division during the war. That would only fuel her imagination...and bring her too close to the truth.

"Oh." She frowned. "So you aren't investigating Jean-Claude's disappearance?"

"Disappearance? Who is Jean-Claude? This is the first I've heard of it." Mr. Pinkerton turned to Mr. Greeley, a question in his tone.

"This is the first I've heard of it also." Mr. Greeley addressed Élan. "You just said he took a position elsewhere. Is there something more I need to know?"

Élan pulled the letter from Lilly's hand and addressed both men. "Our cook, *chef*, Jean-Claude Pascal, packed up and left. We found this letter in his room. It's an offer of a job with the Palmer House in Chicago. Jean-Claude was classically trained as a pastry chef in Paris and London. We were fortunate to have him as long as we did. I'm not surprised he took a better offer, but we have things covered. I've put out inquiries for another cook and, in the meantime, the men are more than pleased with Miss Galloway in charge of the cooking."

Mr. Greeley nodded. "As long as you've got the situation well in hand. Shall we continue the tour?"

"Yes." Élan kept his voice all business, hopefully disguising his intense relief that they weren't going to pursue the matter. "Did you have any other questions about filing?" he asked Mr. Pinkerton. "If not, I'll show you the sleds and ice tank. The men will be done with breakfast in a few minutes, and then you can talk to a few of the sawyers and scalers if you'd like." He pointed to the tool shanty and took a step in that direction, indicating that the men should follow. "Most of them will be heading out of camp right away. We're clearing a new road leading to a stand of timber just northeast of where we cleared last winter. As soon as we have good access to the river, we'll take the whole crew out there. We should be ready to start working it in—"

"What about Jean-Claude?"

Élan's stomach knotted. She was not going to let this go.

Mr. Pinkerton stepped toward Lilly. "It appears you hold a different opinion than Mr. Lamoreaux about what happened to your cook. I'm listening."

Lilly let out a long sigh, her breath crystallizing in the air. It was then he noticed she wasn't wearing her coat. Élan matched her sigh, but while hers was one of relief at finally being heard, his was one of fear that they would listen.

If Lilly was right, and something nefarious had happened to Jean-Claude, anyone within earshot of Élan's last words to Jean-Claude might implicate him in the man's disappearance.

Ceiling-high shelves covered the walls of the tiny office on wheels Élan called the wanigan. Stacks of blankets, bottles of medicine, and tins of tobacco towered above Lilly as she sat in Élan's desk chair, his coat over her shoulders. She'd tried to refuse his offer of the only comfortable seat in the room, but all three men had insisted on sitting on upturned crates and giving her what she could interpret as a place of honor…or an interrogation seat.

"Now…" Only one word from Mr. Greeley, but it set the tone for what she was sure to come. Patronization and condescension. "Tell us why you disagree with Mr. Lamoreaux's assessment."

"This rolling pin is Jean-Claude's most prized possession. He would not purposely leave it behind." She went on to explain how and why he had it. "I think he left it as a sign. Everyone who knows him would know it would be the first thing he would pack if he left willingly. And why, if he was simply taking another job, wouldn't he have talked to Él—Mr. Lamoreaux, or at the very least leave a note?"

"Maybe he just felt uncomfortable," Mr. Greeley said. "The man is a bit…high strung. And the letter from the Palmer House seems to be irrefutable evidence that's where he went."

"Exactly." Élan narrowed his eyes at her when he said it. As if he thought he could silence her with a single look.

That was not going to happen.

"What if the letter was a trap? What if they were simply trying to lure him there so they could turn him in for the bounty?"

"Bounty?" This from Mr. Pinkerton who had, until now, simply sat cradling his chin in his hand. "What bounty?"

Lilly steadied her shaking breath and explained how Jean-Claude had been wrongfully accused of stealing gems from a duchess at the Savoy. "He told me there was a bounty on his head."

Mr. Pinkerton leaned forward, clearly intrigued, but it was Mr. Greeley who spoke. "You knew about this, Mr. Lamoreaux?"

"N-not at first. I hired him at the docks in Green Bay."

"But you kept an escaped suspect in a criminal investigation on my payroll once you found out?" Mr. Greeley's florid face looked like a ripe tomato.

"Sir, no disrespect, but in this business, *as you well know*, we often hire men who have checkered—"

Mr. Greeley held up one hand, palm out, and silenced Élan. "I think we have all of the information we need, Miss Galloway."

Lilly bit her lip. She was being dismissed. Through gritted teeth she said, "Thank you," and stood.

"Wait." It was Mr. Pinkerton's turn to hold up a hand. Lilly sank back onto the wood seat. "You believe Mr. Pascal's story about being wrongly accused of theft. May I ask why you think he was telling the truth?"

"Because..." Why did she believe him? Because he was the first person in Embarrass who paid her any attention? Because he'd taken time to train her when he had nothing to gain from it? "I think...if he was running to escape punishment for a crime he had committed, why wouldn't he change his name? I saw his certificate from the culinary school he attended, so I know he didn't. And why does he tell people about the accusations? Why not come to a new country and start over without leaving any clues to your past?"

William Pinkerton stroked the heavy, dark moustache that made him look like a walrus. After a moment, he nodded. "You make a good point. Did the man have any enemies? Anyone who might wish harm to come to him?"

Élan huffed. "Anyone who ever worked for him."

"Was he especially close with anyone, here or in town?"

"He sometimes went out on a Saturday night with two of my sawyers. I can introduce you to them."

Lilly took a deep breath. She could trust this man, couldn't she? Jean-Claude had his reasons for protecting the identity of his lady friend, but in this time of crisis... "There is a woman he visits every Sunday afternoon. Her name is Mamie. I don't know where she lives."

Mr. Pinkerton nodded again. "I will make some inquiries and see if we can't get to the bottom of this...disappearance."

"Thank you." Though it was possible he was simply humoring her, out of the three men in the room, he was the only one even willing to look her in the eye.

Lilly walked back to the cook shanty. When she entered, Evening Star glanced up from peeling carrots. "Good morning. I didn't know what you'd planned for today, but I had to make my hands busy."

"Carrots are perfect. Sorry I wasn't here. I had a meeting with Mr. Greeley."

"Slim said a famous detective is here. Is he looking for Jean-Claude?"

Lilly took wood from the pile in the corner of the room. "I hope so."

"Do you believe he did not leave because he wanted to?"

"I don't know what I believe anymore." Lilly put two pieces of wood in the oven then spooned dried parsley, thyme, and rosemary into a stone mortar, picked up the heavy pestle, and began mashing and grinding the herbs with far more force than they deserved.

"I did not say this, and now I do not know..." Evening Star lowered her head as her words grew softer and trailed off.

"Tell me. Whatever you know, anything you've heard, might help."

"I do not want to cause trouble for Mr. Lamoreaux."

"You won't. He wants Jean-Claude back, and anything you can say to help solve the mystery will only help him."

Evening Star's face contorted in a grimace. "I think maybe Jean-Claude left because Mr. Lamoreaux screamed at him and said if he was lying, he'd see him…swing at the end of a rope."

❧ CHAPTER EIGHT ❧

Élan sat up and stretched. His loud yawn filled the small cabin. A thin line of light stretched across the view from his window. Above the streak of silver, heavy, dark clouds threatened to open and cover them in deep snow. Or so he hoped. That would make tracking easier. He threw on his jacket, still covered in sawdust from last night when he couldn't sleep. After a quick trip out back, he splashed his face with freezing water from his wash bowl and pulled wool pants and a heavy muslin shirt over his long johns.

He'd skip breakfast this morning, not wanting a confrontation with the stubborn woman he'd hired to make his life easier. Thankfully, he'd squirreled away a few of the sugar cookies she'd made yesterday. Like her, they were soft on the inside, but crunchy on the outside.

After sticking the cookies in the pocket of his red plaid jacket and three letters in his shirt pocket, he grabbed his hat and a pair of mittens then reached for his Winchester. He would have loved a cup of good, strong coffee to start the day, but the cost of seeing Lilly in the kitchen was more than he wanted to pay this morning.

And that was the last thought of Lilly Galloway he would allow until he returned. For the next two hours, except for a brief stop in town, he'd be alone in the woods with nothing but his gun for company. At least he hoped he'd be alone.

The first large, wet snowflakes began falling as he neared the river. In the stillness, he could hear them pelting the leaves. As he breathed in the cold, crisp air, he imagined filling his lungs with all that was good and right and true and exhaling the anxious thoughts that had kept him fighting with his pillow all night.

William Pinkerton had left midafternoon yesterday after covering every inch of the camp, under the guise of being Mr. Greeley's longtime friend who was curious about the workings of a logging camp…all while searching for clues about the men Élan hoped he wouldn't find in the woods.

Until sometime around midnight, it hadn't occurred to him that the two mysteries—the wanted men the Pinkerton Agency sought, and Jean-Claude's disappearance—could be related.

The chill that slithered up his neck had nothing to do with the cold.

He followed the river for two miles until he reached the Main Street bridge. He waited while a horse and carriage clip-clopped across the wooden span then waited again for a wheezing red Runabout to chug past him, blasting its infernal *a-oo-ga* horn at him.

He'd only seen two automobiles around Embarrass. He supposed it was a very different story in Milwaukee. Maybe that was one of the draws that Lilly and her sister longed for. Motorized vehicles and trolley cars, all rushing around, getting people where they wanted to go faster, all while cluttering the peaceful backdrop of nature with noise that could set a man's teeth on edge.

He wanted no part of that life. But what if that was the only way he could have the woman he didn't think he could live without?

Could he reshape himself, become someone he wasn't, for the sake of love?

This was not the time to think about that. He'd left thoughts of Lilly back at camp, and he was determined to keep them there. Just as that conviction formed in his brain, the Galloway Hotel came into view. He took out his pocket watch. Lilly should have left by now. Sweet Pea hadn't been tethered outside the cook shanty when he'd left, but maybe, considering the weather, she'd taken her into the shed.

He picked up his pace, hurrying to get past the hotel undetected on his way to the post office. He breathed a sigh of relief when he slid the letters through the brass slot in the door then turned and walked back past the hotel.

"Mr. Lamoreaux?"

Bette Galloway's voice stopped him. She stood in the open doorway, holding a rug in her hands.

He tipped the bill of his cap. "Morning, ma'am."

"Are you looking for Lilly? She overslept this morning. I don't think she had a good night."

So he wasn't the only one. Though he had no idea what she had to be upset about. She had, after all, garnered an audience with one of the famous Pinkerton brothers. "Sorry to hear that."

"I've been wanting to talk to you." She dropped the rug and walked to the edge of the porch, pulling a shawl tighter around her shoulders. "About Lilly."

Hadn't she said enough? A year ago, when he'd approached her about courting her sister—an unnecessary formality, considering Lilly was almost twenty-two at the time—she'd given him a staunch

59

"No," explaining that she had plans in the works to sell the hotel and take them back to Milwaukee "for Lilly's sake." According to her, "the poor girl has been distraught since she arrived, missing all the city has to offer."

In all that time, he'd heard no more talk of a sale. Maybe she'd changed her mind. "Yes, ma'am?"

"I appreciate you holding up your end of our bargain. Please keep this to yourself, but I have a potential buyer. Lilly and I will be leaving Embarrass by Christmas."

Fumbling with her hairpins, Lilly secured a bun and wrinkled her nose at her unruly bangs. No time to fuss with her usual French twist or to heat a curling iron for those wayward strands. She would simply have to look like a hardworking scullery maid today. Not far from how she felt this morning after three days of galloping between two jobs that required her to be on her feet all day. After grabbing her shawl, she ran down the ornate front stairway.

How could she have slept so late? She'd never owned an alarm clock, never needed one. Even as a child, she was always the first one up. But then, she was usually the first one to turn in and rarely had trouble falling asleep.

This was all Élan's fault. In the six years she'd known him, she'd never felt belittled by him. Why then, yesterday, when she held evidence in her hands that something horrible had likely happened to Jean-Claude, was he treating her like a brainless ninny who'd made up some cockamamie story? What had he been trying to prove to those men? Or hide from them?

In the dining room, she looked around for Bette. Not seeing her, she darted into the kitchen. The pies she'd made yesterday afternoon were crowded together on her worktable, covered with flour sacks. She'd left an equal number of pies on the table in the cook shanty yesterday for the men's supper. Using methods Jean-Claude had learned from his mentor, she'd created a station for herself and each of her coworkers. She mixed the pie dough, Evening Star made the filling, Henry filled the shells, Tobias handled the delicate top crusts, and George was in charge of baking. In two hours, they'd made four custard and five apple pies.

"A little somethin' for the journey, Lilly girl." Dottie held out a biscuit filled with ham.

"Bless you." Lilly kissed her on the cheek, took a bite, and grabbed her coat from the hook by the back door. Still chewing, she managed to say, "Tell Bette goodbye for me."

"Sure 'n I will. Have a blessed day."

With a nod, Lilly ran down the back steps. Snow fell in big, lazy clumps. As she hurried to the livery, flakes landed on her eyelashes. Feeling carefree and childlike, she stuck out her tongue and savored the tiny bites of cold that dissolved quickly.

Billy James, the stable boy, had Sweet Pea saddled and ready. She thanked him profusely. Tomorrow, she'd bring a pie just for him.

As she tore across the bridge, she saw movement in the trees. A flash of plaid. Red and black. Must be her imagination. After a sleepless night of wrestling with her feelings for Élan and her irritation at the way he'd treated her, she was starting to see things. No, not things, *him*.

She rode on, remembering the clamor of voices on Sunday morning when breakfast was late. She prayed Tobias would take charge and start on the French toast and sausage.

Half a mile from camp, she slowed. The road was too rutted here for speed. Sweet Pea nickered, clearly sensing something. Lilly scanned the woods, praying she wouldn't spot a bobcat or wolf. Movement caught her eye. Two men, one leading a horse, wove through the trees. One had a white beard, and the other wore a tattered sack coat and a red bandanna around his neck. Jimmie and Axe. Probably out hunting. By the looks of it, they hadn't been successful. Strange that they'd brought a horse when they were so close to camp. Wouldn't it scare off whatever they were hunting?

The snow was thick when she reached camp. She had no time to spare, but she needed to get Sweet Pea into the horse shed. Thankfully, one of the younger men was there tending the horses and offered to take the animal.

Following the path from the horse shed to the cook shanty meant she'd walk just a couple of yards behind Élan's cabin. Were there windows back there? Could she see in? Even though she was upset with him, curiosity got the best of her, and she veered off the path, taking in everything. Neatly stacked woodpile. Long wooden table up against the cabin, a metal tool carrier on top. She jumped when something swung above her head. She let out a sigh. Just a rope. Just a rope…with a noose at the end. Swinging from a tree. "Why would—"

She let out a shriek as the toe of her boot slammed into something and she launched face-first onto the ground. Slowly, she turned over and sat up. The thing she'd tripped on had some give to it. She leaned forward, gasped, and then forgot how to breathe. She'd fallen on something rolled in a heavy carpet. Something about her height. With a bit of plaid fabric and a shock of dark hair sticking out of one end.

A body. She'd tripped on a dead body. In Élan's backyard!

A scream started deep in her chest, but she had no breath in her lungs. Scrambling on all fours, she slid and scrabbled until she found a foothold. And then she ran. As fast as her legs would carry her.

ᵔᵔ Chapter Nine ᵔᵔ

"How much sugar should I add to the blueberries?" George asked, his voice low, gentle.

Lilly stared at him, not comprehending the question. She still hadn't caught her breath, and she felt like the walls of the kitchen were closing in around her. Blueberries. For the French toast. The dried berries had been simmering on the stove when she stumbled in. The men had started breakfast, and none of them had chastised her for being late. One look at her dirt-streaked coat and disheveled hair, and they'd known something had happened.

Tobias had asked if she was hurt.

"No. I just tripped." *On a dead body.* "I'm f-fine." Her teeth had chattered so hard she could barely get the words out. She'd scrubbed her hands until they were bright red then poured a cup of hot water for tea, but she trembled too much to measure tea leaves, so she'd settled for hot water to warm her insides. Now, it took all her concentration to cut thick slices of bread for the French toast.

George had asked her something. Blueberries. How could she think about blueberries when Jean-Claude's body lay stiff and frozen just yards away? She gripped the edge of the table and bent down as stars swam before her eyes. Her breath still came in short, ragged gasps. Her thoughts seemed mired in quicksand. What was the question? Blueberries. "Two. Two cups of sugar should be enough. Taste it. After."

The sharp knife crunched through the crust then sliced through the soft, white bread. *Crunch. Slice. Crunch.* Had Jean-Claude suffered? Hanging was quick, wasn't it? Instant.

Had Élan given him time to repent, to make peace with God before stringing him up? Why had he not reported whatever Jean-Claude had done to the sheriff, leaving the punishment in the hands of the law? This was not the Wild West, where no law existed and it was every man for himself.

No matter what Jean-Claude had done, Élan did not have the right or the authority to sentence him to death. How could he have done it? How could he have taken a man's life with his own hands?

Was she losing her mind? How could she have been so wrong about him? How had she let her heart mislead her?

But maybe it wasn't. Maybe her wild imagination was creating a scenario her heart rebelled against. She did know Élan. She knew him to be kind and trustworthy. And yet, he was the one charged with protecting the men. If Jean-Claude had done something that put the camp at risk, or if he'd threatened Élan... That must be it. Self-defense.

Or maybe it wasn't a body after all. Maybe she should go back and take another look. But what else could it be? The plaid fabric... There'd been a button on it, she was sure. A shirt sleeve. And hair... the same color as Jean-Claude's.

Why hadn't he buried the body? How could he simply roll it in a carpet and leave it on the ground where animals...

She stifled a sob and squeezed her eyes shut to block out the vision.

She'd told Evening Star she had a feeling the men were up to something. She didn't believe Mr. Pinkerton had just stopped by for a friendly visit. Did he already know about Jean-Claude? Were he and Mr. Greeley in on it? Maybe Élan wasn't guilty, at least not in the way she'd thought. Maybe he hadn't taken matters into his own hands but had been deputized by Mr. Pinkerton. Did Mr. Pinkerton have that kind of authority? And why, then, hadn't they removed the body?

Her entire frame shook. She had to tell someone. But who? Not the one person she'd thought she could trust more than anyone else. Not Élan.

After breakfast, when Evening Star got here, she'd leave. She'd ride to town and get the sheriff. But for now, she needed to act as if nothing was wrong. She needed to paste a smile on her face and go about being in charge of the Soleil Rouge camp kitchen. For the last time? Would there even be a camp if the foreman had killed the chef? Would the camp she was trying to save close *because* of her? Would the sawmill close and people leave and Embarrass turn into a ghost town *because of her*?

Thoughts spun like leaves in a whirlwind. She pulled syrup pitchers from a shelf as if her world hadn't been upended and a man wasn't lying dead not far from where she stood.

Maybe she should keep quiet. No one knew. Unless they had a January thaw, the body would stay frozen until spring. That would give the loggers time to finish their cutting and send the logs downriver to the mill. The town would be saved.

Over the summer, there'd be time to reorganize, to hire a new foreman. But what about a head cook right now? Could Tobias handle the job? Surely she couldn't stay on here, keeping her mouth shut and Élan's secret to herself while seeing him every day. No. She wasn't sure how she could ever look him in the eye again. Could never, ever, trust him—or her own instincts. But if she quit, he would be suspicious. Would he come after her?

Through the closed door, she could hear the men entering the dining room. Boots scuffed, the floor creaked, and chairs scraped.

Élan had not stopped in for his morning coffee.

She picked up a syrup tin and set it on the table. As lightly and casually as she could manage, she said, "Haven't seen Mr. Lamoreaux this morning. Was he in for his breakfast before I arrived?"

All three men shook their heads.

Had it really been him she'd seen just outside of town after all? Sneaking around in the woods? Running? But he was heading toward the camp, not away from it. And…a detail surfaced that hadn't registered in her hurry to get here.

He'd been carrying a gun.

For the next hour, she moved without thinking. She mixed biscuit dough then rolled and cut, rolled and cut, working like a machine, like the hay baler she'd seen at the state fair that produced square bales, one after the other.

By the time Evening Star arrived, she had the day's menu written down and everything lined up for flaggins and supper. "I have some errands to run in town." She addressed the four people now staring at the paper that trembled in her hand like a spring leaf. "I think you can all carry on without me."

Not waiting for an answer, she grabbed her dirt-streaked coat and left.

The snow was slowing, finally. Élan rubbed the small of his back then bent and swiped the blade through the snow to clean it. He hoped he'd get a couple of hours later this afternoon to finish what he'd started.

Back in his cabin, he washed his hands and took off his shirt. Despite the cold, he had sweated through two layers. He'd just put on a clean shirt when he heard horses. Several of them, coming toward the camp at a gallop. Strange. The rutted road wasn't suitable for that kind of speed. He slipped into his coat and stepped out onto the porch.

"Sheriff?" Did the man have news? Had they found the men Pinkerton was looking for? "What brings you out this way?"

"Raise your hands where I can see them." Sheriff Wagner leveled a pistol. Without taking his eyes off Élan, he dismounted.

"What…?" Élan lifted his hands to shoulder height. "What's going on?"

The sheriff gestured with the gun. "There's blood on your coat."

"Been hunting."

"Uh-huh." The sheriff turned his head, but not his gaze, a bit to the left. "Where is it?" He spoke over his shoulder, to one of the other riders.

"Behind the cabin," said a small, quavering voice that cut through Élan's gut quicker than if she'd used the steel blade of the Green River knife he'd just stuck in the table out back.

"Lilly? What—"

"Quiet," the sheriff commanded. "Keep your hands up. Step down from the porch and take us to the body."

"The...what?" Had he trespassed on someone's property this morning? Still, who would call the sheriff? Why not confront him personally? He'd gladly turn "the body" over to some hair-splitting, tied-in-knots new landowner who didn't know how things worked around here. And what did Lilly have to do with this?

He walked down the steps, keeping his hands in sight, and turned the corner. "Come on, Sheriff, haven't you better things to do with your time?" He didn't recognize the young man with them. His silver star was shiny, brand-new looking. Maybe this was a training session for him. That had to be it. Élan grinned and shook his head. He could play along.

"Nothing better to do than arrest a man for murder."

Élan stumbled. His hands went down to catch himself. He heard Wagner cock his gun. He righted himself quickly and shoved his hands back in the air, higher this time. *Murder?* Was this all a joke on the new deputy? He'd read about hazings, ritual humiliation used as an initiation in some fraternal organizations. The poor man.

Élan rounded the rear corner of the cabin and pointed. "There she is."

"*She?*" The deputy's voice wobbled.

Élan stifled a laugh as the two men and one crunchy young woman stared up at the deer hanging by a rope from the oak behind his cabin. "She...as in doe. I'm guessing about a three-year-old. I saw a buck, but didn't get a good shot, so—"

"On the ground." Lilly's voice was not nearly as weak as it had been moments ago. "Rolled in the carpet."

"No!" The word escaped before he could stop it. A gun barrel stabbed into his ribs.

"Unroll it." The sheriff spoke to the deputy, who immediately stepped over the carpet and began unrolling it until the thing lay there, exposed, spoiling everything.

Lilly gasped, then crumpled to her knees.

⌒ CHAPTER TEN ⌒

Cold, wet snow seeped through her coat and her wool stockings as she knelt on the ground, staring at…what?

Wood. Not skin. A beaver skin cap. Not hair. A ripped and dirty shirt sleeve turned into a work rag. She leaned forward then gasped again. Half tree stump, half…moose head? With a… Another gasp. A butterfly on the tip of its nose. It wasn't finished. Only one antler. But… It was the most beautiful thing she'd ever seen. And here she'd… "Oh, Moose. I'm so, so, so sorry. I thought you'd…killed… hung…Jean-Claude." A tear slid down her cheek as she finally found the courage to look up at him.

"*What?*" Astonishment froze Élan's face. The sheriff lowered his gun. The deputy took his hand from his holster and covered his mouth as a laugh sputtered out. And then the sheriff joined him. After a long, horrible, humiliating moment, Élan finally moved. His arms lowered, and a howl burst from his lips. Laughter. She knelt in cold, wet snow, her face hot with embarrassment, and All. Three. Men. Laughed at her!

"Lilly." Still laughing, Élan dropped onto his knees in front of her and put his hands on her shoulders.

She ducked her head. She couldn't look at him, not this close, not when she'd just made a complete fool of herself.

"Guess we're done here." Amusement danced in the sheriff's tone.

"Thank you for doing your duty, sir," Élan said, mirth coating his words. "We know we're safe with you around."

Footsteps crunched in snow, but the laughter continued, echoing in the trees, as they mounted their horses and rode off.

"Look at me, Papillon. Please." Élan's voice was serious now, low and husky, tender.

She couldn't. She covered her face with her hands and shook her head. His fingertips, calloused and warm, lifted her chin until she had no choice but to look into his eyes. "I'm such a dolt."

This time his laugh was soft. "But you are an adorable dolt."

She sniffed, and finally smiled. "You're mean."

"I've been told that before. But at least I'm not a murderer."

Lilly groaned and pulled away. The forgiveness in his eyes was too much. He stood and reached down for her hands and helped her up. For a moment, she thought he might draw her into his arms, but of course he didn't. But he did rest his hand lightly on the small of her back.

"Let's get you inside and warm."

Inside? Inside the cabin? Just the two of them? What if the men were watching? But instead of steering her around the corner, he guided her to the cook shanty.

Partway there, she stopped. "I heard you yelled at Jean-Claude and threatened to hang him."

A loud sigh rushed from Élan's lungs. "I yelled all right, and I said if he didn't straighten up, I'd see him hang. I did not say *I* would hang him."

"You accused him of lying."

Another sigh, this one long and quiet. "I do not want to disparage the little man in your eyes. I know he is your friend, and I suppose he has his good qualities. But he is not always truthful, and I can't abide that in a man." He opened the cook shanty door and stepped aside.

The dining room was empty, and the same feeling of reverence swept over her as he ushered her to a bench near the long woodstove that reminded her of a giraffe. She sat, and he added two split logs to the red coals in the belly of the stove. Then he sat beside her.

"The moose...you carved it?"

"Yes. Still making it. It was supposed to be a surprise. For your birthday."

He remembered her birthday? Tears stung her eyes. "I love it. And you couldn't possibly have surprised me more than by leaving it out for me to trip over." She angled on the bench to face him. "I know it sounds ridiculous, but you have to know how it looked to me. How it felt. The carpet made it feel...spongy." She wrinkled her nose. "And there was hair sticking out!"

His chuckle shook the bench. "I didn't wrap it correctly after working on it late last night, and I didn't want it to get wet, so I stuffed my hat in the end."

Lilly shook her head. "I suppose the whole camp will know about this by noon."

"They won't hear it from me."

She gazed at him, taking in every angle, every line and whisker. How she loved that face. Would he ever come to see her as more than a silly, flitting butterfly? Not if she kept doing foolish stunts that drew attention to her lack of judgment and common sense. "Thank you."

They sat in silence for several minutes. "I love this place when it's empty," she said. "It feels…sacred. I suppose that sounds silly."

"Not at all." He seemed to hesitate, as if he wasn't sure he wanted to say what was on his mind. "I often come here to pray."

Her heart did a little hop-skip. She knew he was a church-going man, but she had no idea he took his faith seriously.

"My father is a minister," he said. "He wanted me to follow in his footsteps."

Lilly held her breath, waiting for him to continue, not wanting to break the intimacy of the moment. They'd never talked like this. "But you didn't want that?"

"It wasn't ministering or preaching that I rejected. It was the rest of it. The politics and prejudice. My father let himself be controlled by wealthy parishioners who wanted things done their way, and that sometimes meant not allowing someone they didn't approve of to enter the doors of the church. I had two years of seminary and couldn't take any more. I have to believe Jesus had something else in mind for His Church."

She nodded. "I experienced some of that in Milwaukee. Sometimes it felt like we just went to church to be seen in new hats. I've often wondered what it was like in the first century when Christians met in homes. Wouldn't it feel more like meeting with family than like a fashion parade?" She covered her mouth with her hand. "I'm sorry. That was overly critical."

"That was honest. I know there were many in the church I grew up in who had a genuine love for Christ, but the fashion-parade picture fits many of the others. Here, in this room, or out in the woods, a person can worship unhindered, the way I think it's supposed to be."

"What happens here on Sundays? I know you have services."

"We have a traveling preacher once a month. In between, we meet midafternoon to sing hymns. Winnipeg and Axe play a pretty mean fiddle. Jimmie and Cordwood usually join in on their harmonicas. And sometimes I…say a word or two." His cheeks reddened.

"You mean you preach?" She grinned at him.

"I…guess you could call it that."

"Then I'm coming on Sunday. That is, if you allow silly butterflies at your services."

He laughed then pressed his arm against hers for just a moment. "You are so much more than a silly butterfly, Papillon."

Élan sank onto his desk chair and rubbed his face with both hands. He was beyond tired, but he needed to start securing things in the wanigan. They would be moving it in three days. The easy season was coming to a close. Soon it would be ten-hour days, starting at first light and ending at dusk. They'd stop long enough to down sandwiches and coffee at noon then forge on. Even though he was no longer a sawyer, he still pitched in wherever he could, which meant he would be exhausted at the end of each day.

"I'm getting too old for this." Maybe it was time to make the change he'd been saving for. What that looked like, he wasn't exactly sure. He wanted a job where he could make a difference, help people, but it had to be something that was drastically different than what his father was doing.

His thirtieth birthday loomed on the horizon. That wasn't so old, but his mind and body felt it today. Maybe it was more that his spirit felt tired after yesterday. He kept reliving the moment when he'd knelt in front of Lilly, lifting her chin until she gazed into his eyes. It had taken all his strength not to kiss her.

How would she have reacted? Would she have returned his kiss? Or would she have pushed him away?

It made no difference. He couldn't do this to her, or to himself. Any confession of feelings would only make it harder to say goodbye. She'd be gone by Christmas. Back to culture and civility, snooty women and pompous men and societal norms that kept people in line, albeit often miserable. "Lord, why have you allowed me to have these feelings if they are for naught?" he whispered aloud.

When no answer came, he picked up the stack of mail one of the men had set on his desk yesterday, mail he hadn't taken the time to sort. Several letters for the men, one smelling of lilacs, and a newspaper. He spread the *Clintonville Tribune* on his desk, intending to skim the headlines and take it back to his cabin to read tonight.

On the front page, the third column from the left, near the top, four words grabbed his attention.

Train Robbed at Buckbee

On November 29 around midnight, a Chicago & North-western train was held up at Buckbee, and the conductor was robbed by two masked men. As the train began to leave the station, two men rose from the darkness at the side of *the track and boarded a passenger car. Both men kept guns trained on passengers until they found the conductor on the third car. One man held a gun on the passengers while the other took from the conductor his gold watch and his cash, amounting, it is estimated, to about $50. They then held the conductor at gunpoint and forced him to lead them to the baggage car, where he turned over the cashbox enroute to two iron mines in Oneida County. The box contained the payroll for more than one hundred men. The robbers then jumped from the car and disappeared in the darkness.*

There were only a few passengers aboard, and they were not harmed. Passengers and the conductor reported that both men were of average height and wore brown dusters. The shorter, stockier man had a black cloth over his face and a hatchet strapped to his back with "HB" stamped on the blade. The other, taller and leaner, had a dirty red bandanna around his neck, as well as one covering his face. One reliable source said this could be the same pair that robbed a C&NW train near Shawano last month, which could mean the thieves reside in the area. Be warned, these men are armed and dangerous.

Élan closed his eyes. He'd been dreading this. It was inevitable the news would get out to the public, but why did they have to sensationalize the story by adding unsourced speculation and the "armed and dangerous" warning?

William Pinkerton had done a meticulous inventory of the toolshed, looking for the hatchet with *HB* on the blade. They hadn't found it. Élan had seen that maker's mark in a magazine. Hults Bruk. A Swedish company.

He had half a dozen men from Sweden in his crew.

Pinkerton had told him to ask around, but in a way that wouldn't tip off the robbers. He'd brought it up casually to the two filers and had gotten nothing but blank stares. That did not, however, mean they knew nothing.

Then again, there were other camps around, and it wasn't just loggers who carried hatchets. But until the robbers were captured, he'd continue to be on edge, wondering every day if he rubbed shoulders with two men who might be "armed and dangerous."

At least one reassuring thing had come out. Eyewitnesses said the men were of average height.

The little Frenchman was not one of them.

⌒ CHAPTER ELEVEN ⌒

Lilly finished her baking in the hotel kitchen on Thursday afternoon with an hour to spare before they needed to prepare for the supper crowd. She took off her apron and walked out into the dining room. This space, when empty, didn't give her the same feeling as the dining room at the camp, and yet it was a welcoming place. Homey and comfortable with the lace curtains Lilly had recommended when she first moved here letting in light that reflected on the high, white-painted pressed-tin ceiling. Navy and gold damask wallpaper and crystal teardrops hanging from the gold and glass gaslit fixtures gave a touch of elegance. A fire, burning low and red, cast a rose-hued glow about the room.

She peeked into the parlor. With its carved cherrywood fireplace and rich floral rug in dark blues and tans with threads of gold, it was her favorite room in the hotel. The tufted blue sofas and wingback chairs that faced the fireplace lacked the gilt framing Bette would have loved but maintained the air of quality she desired while still being comfortable enough for Lilly's tastes.

Two of their permanent guests, Mr. and Mrs. Tremont, read by the fire in the parlor. Mr. Louis, who sold some kind of miracle cleaning product, dozed in a rocking chair, a newspaper almost covering his face.

Bette was nowhere to be seen. It was rare, but not unheard of, for her to take an afternoon nap. Lilly walked back into the kitchen, breathing in the comforting aroma of Dottie's famous chicken soup simmering in a large pot on the stove. Thick egg noodles hung from strings stretched across the room. Her stomach growled. All she'd eaten that day was a piece of bread with a slice of ham. But right now, she was more tired than hungry. This chance to put her feet up was a rare treat. What she needed was a good cup of tea.

When the water was ready, she opened the pantry door. The soft sounds of snoring greeted her. Dottie was sound asleep on the cot she kept at the back of the pantry in the winter for those nights when walking home was too treacherous. Or times like this, when she'd finished her work and had a bit of time to spare.

Holding her breath, Lilly lifted the cover off what Dottie called the biscuit crock and retrieved one of the oatmeal raisin cookies Lilly had made last night when her mind was spinning too fast to head for bed.

Back in the kitchen, she spooned tea leaves into her mother's Staffordshire teapot with its Chinese-inspired, painted motifs and then took a matching cup from the cupboard. She'd brought very few things from home when she'd moved, making these that much more treasured.

As the tea steeped, she unlaced her boots and slipped them off. Bette would be horrified, of course. Ladies did not appear outside of their bedchambers without footwear. But Bette was not around. She padded across the wood floor on feet that thanked her for their free-dom, stopping at the small desk in the corner to sift through the mail. Their first Christmas postcard had arrived. She'd barely had time to think about Christmas. Over the summer, she had knitted a sweater for Dottie, but she still needed something for Bette, who was always so hard to gift, and something for Élan.

The thought brought her back to the moose with the butterfly on its nose. What did it mean? Was it just a silly gift, or did it have a deeper meaning? What was the significance of the butterfly? Of course, it represented her, but had he positioned it on the nose to symbolize closeness, to say something about his feelings for her, or was it supposed to mean that she was as pesky and annoying as an insect?

The December issue of *The Ladies' Home Journal* sat on top of this week's *Clintonville Tribune*. She picked up both and, with her teacup in the other hand, took a chair at the table, elevating her feet on another chair. Another never-do thing.

The magazine cover depicted a sketch of four women decorating a red-painted door for Christmas. They wore the latest dress styles...high collars, tight sleeves, skirts too form-fitting across the hips to allow for enjoying pie, and blousy bodices that made them all look like bullfrogs with puffed-out chests.

Inside, she read every page, starting with topics for future stories, which included one about Helen Keller's life "Written Entirely by the Wonderful Girl Herself." She read a story by Rudyard Kipling then perused advertisements for Royal Seal rolled oats, Packer's Tar Soap, and Walter Baker & Co's chocolate and cocoa. Her tea was almost gone. She had just started reading a story titled "Christmas Eve on Lonesome, A Tale of the Kentucky Mountains," when Bette swooped down the back stairs. Her face was flushed, her eyes red.

Lilly lifted her feet from the chair, sat up straight, and closed the magazine. "Is something wrong?"

"Not something. Everything." Bette looked down at *The Ladies' Home Journal* cover and let out a very uncharacteristic wail. Pressing a handkerchief to her mouth, she pointed at the women in the sketch. "Th-that was supposed to be us." Her shoulders shook in a sob.

"What do you mean?" Lilly pushed her chair back and stood then put her arms awkwardly around her sister. Bette was not a very huggable person. In seconds, she pulled out of Lilly's arms.

"I tried. I thought it was a sure thing, but those train robbers ruined everything!" Another wail.

"Train robbers? Here, sit down. I made tea."

Surprisingly, in the middle of a workday, Bette complied. Lilly retrieved another cup and filled both. She had a feeling she would need a second cup for this. "Now, take a few sips and start from the beginning."

Bette did as she was told. When her ragged breathing slowed, she tugged the newspaper out from under the magazine and pointed to an article above the fold.

Train Robbed at Buckbee. "That's only a few miles from here," Lilly murmured, then read the article. When she reached the last few sentences, she felt lightheaded. *The shorter, stockier man had a hatchet....the other, taller and leaner, had a dirty red bandanna around his neck...could be the same pair that robbed a C&NW train near Shawano...could mean the thieves reside in the area...armed and dangerous.*

Two men. One stocky, the other tall and lean. One with a red bandanna around his neck.

Forcing her attention back on Bette, Lilly tried to make sense of what her sister had said. "What did the bank robbers ruin? For us, I mean."

"Everything." Bette gave a very unladylike hiccup. "I had a buyer for the hotel, but when he read—"

"You *what*?"

"A man...from Green Bay. He owns several hotels, and he wanted to buy ours. Lilly..." She grabbed Lilly's arm. "This was our ticket out of this horrible place."

"Horrible place?" Lilly pushed back her chair, stood, and then began pacing. "This is our home. This is where our friends are, our church. People love our food, we hardly ever have vacancies, and..." *Moose.* How could she leave him?

She couldn't. That was all there was to it. If Bette wanted to go back to Milwaukee, she could do it without her. She would stay and...get a job. Maybe the new owner would keep her... Wait. "He reneged on the deal?"

"Yes." Bette wept into her hankie. "He sent a telegram this afternoon. He stayed here in May and thought Embarrass was such a pretty place, quiet and tranquil he called it, but now he says he was mistaken and it is"—she pulled the tan telegram out of her apron pocket—"'still part of the vast untamed wilderness,' and he couldn't recommend it to guests."

Lilly settled back in her chair, her pulse returning to normal. "I'm sure someone else will come along," she said, her voice weak. For Bette's sake she hoped her sister would find a way to return to the city. *Just please, Lord, not before I figure out how I'm going to support myself when she leaves.*

Another wail. "N-not before Christmas." Bette tapped the magazine with a damp finger. "I wanted this, you and me in a sweet little apartment downtown, maybe on Wells Street, walking distance from the Pabst Theater and shopping and restaurants. We'd be back in society, where we could both meet real men. Men who don't spit tobacco in public, who wear top hats and cologne and starched white shirts that stay white and trim their moustaches and *bathe*. Men who tip their hats and know how to treat a lady and would never..."

As Bette prattled on about men who sounded anything but "real," Lilly's mind went to the newspaper article.

Red bandanna. And a hatchet, which was just an axe with a shorter handle. Who carried hatchets around with them? Loggers.

Were Axe and Jimmie the train robbers?

Friday. Breakfast was done, and there was only one more day until Sunday. Every bone in Lilly's body longed for a Sabbath rest. Not that working at the hotel on their busiest day was restful, but at least the only person looking over her shoulder would be her sister. Not the lumberjack she'd been sure was going to kiss her while she was on her knees in the snow.

Élan had stopped in the kitchen this morning just long enough to grab a plate of food and a cup of coffee and be on his way. He didn't say why he was in a hurry, but he was out the door before she had a chance to talk to him alone about the train robbers. She'd have to try to catch him before she left camp.

She dumped a mound of chopped carrots and parsnips into the massive pot of broth on the stove and looked around. Evening Star and the three men were finally working like a team. With her part done, Lilly picked up Jean-Claude's cookbook and began searching for something new to make with venison. They had carrots, winter squash, cabbage, potatoes, garlic, and onions. It would have to be some kind of stew. Something that could simmer all day to tenderize the meat. Onion and garlic would help with that too. She found a recipe for cabbage soup that called for smoked pork. She wanted to conserve the meat George and Henry had smoked a few days ago. That would keep, but the venison Élan had just butchered would last only as long as the temperature stayed below freezing.

The image of the deer hanging from the noose she thought he'd used to kill Jean-Claude made her face heat all over again. She forced her thoughts back to supper. The meat and broth would be ready by suppertime, and all Tobias would need to do would be to add the chopped cabbage and let it cook for half an hour. She turned a page in the cookbook, looking for inspiration for the next day.

She found recipes for chestnut soup and cold vichyssoise. She was quite sure the men would not be pleased with either. Lobster bisque required something most people in Wisconsin had never seen, let alone tasted. Pumpkin, mushroom, and carrot soup were all possibilities, as long as she added chunks of meat. She'd heard of people who ate only vegetables, but she'd be laughed out of the cook shanty if she dared serve a meatless meal.

She turned another page. A folded paper was glued to the top. She opened it and stared at the letterhead.

The Mahl Hotel
612 Main Street
Shawano, Wisconsin

Beneath the address was a handwritten recipe for beef bourguignon. She read the ingredients, especially interested in the herbs. Garlic, thyme, bay leaves…

At the bottom of the page was a note.

> *16 Octobre 1901*
> *Très cher Jean,*
> *C'est ma joie de partager nos recettes familiales avec vous. Mon cœur se réjouit de vous avoir à nouveau proche.*
> *Tout mon amour,*
> *Mamie*

If only her French were fluent enough to quickly translate. *Très cher* was a term of endearment. Dearest Jean. *C'est ma joie*…it is my joy. Then something about recipes. Family recipes. *Cœur* was heart. My heart. She couldn't figure out the rest of the last sentence, but she was sure about the closing. All my love, Mamie.

As recently as two months ago, Mamie had stayed at a hotel in Shawano. Since Jean-Claude was able to visit her every Sunday, she lived close. It was likely she was a permanent resident at the Mahl Hotel.

Lilly closed the book and walked to the window. The clouds were low, promising more snow, but it wasn't windy. She turned and stared at the four people preparing for the next meal. All she needed to do was give them instructions. They could handle the rest without her.

Sweet Pea could get her to Shawano by noon.

There was just one thing she needed to do before she left.

CHAPTER TWELVE

"Good girl." Lilly patted Sweet Pea's neck as the snow began to fall in earnest. "We're almost there."

Were they? It hadn't occurred to her until they were heading northwest that she'd never ridden twelve miles on horseback alone. Or…ever. The only thing she knew for sure was that she needed to follow the train track as closely as possible. And she needed to leave Shawano in time to get back to the road she and Sweet Pea were familiar with before dark.

The wind picked up, driving snowflakes under the collar of her coat. A train whistle floated through the snow, sounding both lonely and adventurous.

She spotted a tiny cabin far off the road, on a bit of a rise. She guessed she was about halfway to Shawano, at least five miles from civilization. The word *lonely* surfaced again. What would cause someone to want to live in such isolation?

Not far from the cabin, she passed a tree with a broken limb swinging in the wind like a pendulum, adding to the eerie desolation.

Several miles later, as Sweet Pea clopped across the bridge over the Wolf River, the clouds thinned enough to reveal the pale orb of the sun straight overhead. A horse and carriage passed her, the driver with his head down as he rode into the driving snow. Finally, she passed a house, and then another, until they were crowded together, built close to the street. She passed a hardware store and mercantile. It only took her a few minutes to spot THE MAHL HOTEL printed in large black letters on the side of a two-story white clapboard building.

Lilly slowed Sweet Pea as they neared. What would she say when she walked in? Would they simply tell her what room Mamie was in, or would they send someone to inquire if she was receiving guests? What kind of a woman was she? How long had she and Jean-Claude known each other, and why had they never married?

As she dismounted in front of the hotel, a gentleman in a bowler hat stepped out and held the door for her. The lobby was larger and more open than the Galloway, but much darker. Burgundy velvet curtains with gold fringe shrouded the windows. Large potted plants with long, tapered leaves resembled giant spiders.

"May I help you, ma'am?"

The deep, male voice startled her. She turned to the man behind the ornately carved desk. "Yes." Her voice quavered. She had to sound confident, in control of all her faculties. "I'm looking for a woman named Mamie. I believe she is a resident here."

"I'm sorry, there is no one here by that name."

Lilly stared at him. Had she come all this way on a silly whim? "I'm a friend of her…friend. Jean-Claude Pascal." Her face flushed. He'd just told her Mamie wasn't here.

"Ah!" The man brightened. "Yes, she is very worried about him."

"She…Mamie?"

His amused smile widened. "Her name is Genevieve. Do you have news about Jean-Claude?"

"Y-yes." Far more questions than news, but if it would gain her an audience with Genevieve…

"Right this way." He stepped from behind the desk and led her up a curved stairway with pineapple finials on the newel posts. Their steps were muffled by the burgundy and green runner. He stopped at a door with a gold number six on it and knocked. "Mrs. Duval, you have a visitor. A friend of Jean-Claude."

Mrs.? She was a married woman?

The door opened, and a diminutive woman wearing a dark red dress trimmed in lace smiled up at them. A woman with beautiful silvery-white hair. "Come in. Come in. You know my grandson?"

"Please, dear. Call me Genevieve. I suppose that was confusing. Mamie is a name French children sometimes call their *grand-mère*." Jean-Claude's grandmother sat in a straight-back chair with a needlepoint cushion and gestured to a floral-print settee. "I feel as though I already know you. Jean has talked so much about his protégé."

"He has?" She wanted to say it was strange that Jean-Claude had never given any details about her, but she knew why he hadn't. He was protecting her in case his past caught up with him. Which it likely had.

"All the time. He even brought me one of your butterfly pies. Dutch apple. It was divine."

"Thank you." Lilly rubbed a brass upholstery tack with the tip of her finger. "Did he come to see you last Sunday?"

"No. He sent a note. It was in his hand, but it did not sound like him. He said he was fine, just busy at the camp and couldn't get away for a while. Is that...true?"

"No. He...left the camp." She considered suggesting he may have taken a job in Chicago, but that would not be comforting. Surely, he would never have left without saying goodbye to her. "We don't know where he is. I was hoping you might shed some light for us."

Genevieve, for all her poise and elegance, appeared ready to crumble. She pressed trembling lips together and shook her head.

"Do you know anyone who might wish harm to come to him?" Lilly phrased it just like Mr. Pinkerton had.

Again, the tight lips and shake of silver-white curls. Lilly couldn't tell if Genevieve was simply trying to keep her composure or was clamping her mouth shut to keep from saying something.

"I know a little about his past, the trouble at the Savoy. Do you think anyone from England could have come looking for him?"

A tiny sob escaped Genevieve's tight lips, and her pale gray eyes shimmered with tears. "It has been my greatest fear since he arrived. I have told him many times that we cannot outrun our pasts. I pray for him often. I raised him, you know."

"I didn't. What was he like as a child?"

"When he was six years old, he and his mother came to live with me in Paris because Jean-Claude's father was here, fighting in the War Between the States. He was vehemently opposed to slavery, and it did not hurt that the Union offered an alluring fee for foreign enlistees. He was killed at the Battle of Cold Harbor in 1864. Two weeks after the news reached us, my daughter succumbed to cholera, leaving my sweet little Jean an orphan."

"Oh." Lilly's eyes stung. "That may explain why he had such compassion for me when I first arrived in Embarrass. I lost my parents to smallpox six years ago."

Genevieve nodded. "He has such a big heart. He went through his time of rebellion, but God used it to shape him into a kind, gentle man."

Lilly swallowed hard. She could imagine Jean-Claude being tender and caring to his grandmother, but kind and gentle would not be adjectives the men who worked under him would use. "Rebellion?"

"Like many boys, he had to push the limits." Her face crinkled in amusement. "He was well known by the Paris police. He had a reputation for being the slyest pickpocket in our neighborhood."

Why was the woman smiling? If he had a criminal record in Paris, it was no wonder the authorities in London had no trouble believing him guilty of thievery.

"Then he discovered cooking…and everything changed. An old friend of mine, a restaurateur, hired him to clear tables in his establishment. He did it as a favor to me, to keep Jean off the streets. Little did he know, my Jean had a gift for combining flavors and textures and creating art in the kitchen. One day, when two of the cooks were ill, Jean stepped in and created a masterpiece with…"

Genevieve's stories went on and on. And all the while, Lilly watched the snow piling up on the trees outside the window and wondered if the old adage "once a thief, always a thief" held truth.

Feeling lighter than he had in weeks, Élan left the toolshed and walked toward the wanigan. He'd just hired four more men, all with experience. That took a weight off his shoulders. All he needed to do the rest of the day was take a wagon into town to pick up a few supplies. Sooner rather than later would be smart. Though he had a good two hours until sundown, they'd gotten at least three inches of snow already. The sky still looked heavy, and the wind was picking up, creating small drifts that curled like miniature whitecaps on Lake Superior.

He stepped into the wanigan and walked between crates to his desk to get the list he'd made this morning. But the first thing he spotted was a telegram envelope with *Lamoreaux, Soleil Rouge* scrawled on the front in a feathery hand. He tore it open.

Suspects spotted near Belle Plaine. Sheriff notified. Be on lookout.

Élan sat down. Maybe this was good news. The men hadn't fled the area like they feared. Maybe this would all be over soon.

The first year he was at the camp, there was a mountain lion prowling nearby. He'd seen the prints with his own eyes. Five inches across. The men who had spotted it slinking among the trees claimed it was more than three feet high at the shoulders and had to weigh more than two hundred pounds. They'd all been jumpy that winter, always on the alert, guns at the ready. That was how he felt now.

He set the telegram on the desk. A folded paper sat on top of the supply list. When he opened it, the first thing he saw was the signature.

Élan,

I have reason to believe that two of the men you shared my secret recipe with on Sunday morning are the ones who were on the train. Keep a close eye on them, but be careful.

Also, I am going to see a woman at the Mahl Hotel in Shawano
today who may have information on the other man.
   Lilly

Élan read the words over. And then again. Why the strange wording? It didn't sound like Lilly. *Two of the men you shared my secret recipe with…* He didn't know any of her secret recipes. Even if he did, why would he share them? He rubbed his forehead with his thumb and index finger. *On Sunday.* He'd had his usual breakfast at the hotel. Eggs, fried potatoes, bacon…and chess pie! The recipe Lilly had invented by tripping with a cup of coffee in her hand and spilling into the cocoa and sugar. But he hadn't shared her recipe. He'd merely enjoyed it. His eyes widened. He enjoyed it—*shared* it—with Axe, Jimmie, and Jean-Claude. Two of them were on… His blood ran cold. *On the train.* He thought back to the description he'd read in the paper. Axe and Jimmy? He couldn't let himself believe they were capable of such a thing. And yet…

And what about a woman…in Shawano? Today? She'd gone there *today*? How? Had someone gone with her?

Belle Plaine, where the robbers had been spotted, was about four miles northwest. On the way to Shawano.

Smashing his cap back on his head, he strode to the door, whipped it open, and jumped down, not bothering with the steps. Taking off at a run, he reached the cook shanty just as Evening Star was leaving.

"Where is she? Lilly. Is she here?"

"Here?" Evening Star narrowed her eyes at him.

"She left a note saying she was going to Shawano. What time did she leave?"

"Earlier than usual. Right after breakfast. She didn't say where she was going."

He nodded, turned, and ran toward the horse shed. There was no point in looking for Axe and Jimmy. They would have left with the other sawyers right after breakfast. Where had they been at the time of the robbery? His head hurt with trying to remember anything suspicious.

He couldn't dwell on that now. At any minute the snow could become blinding. Was Lilly on her way home? Had she made it back to the hotel? If he rode into town to find out, he'd lose precious time. He trusted Sweet Pea's instincts, but even a horse could get lost when visibility decreased. And the weather was the least of his worries. A woman alone…

"Father, what do I do? Should I go after her?"

At that moment, Lollipop nickered. God had once spoken through a donkey. Could he not send a message through a horse?

Whether or not Lollipop was acting at the Lord's behest, he was going to saddle her and find Lilly before it was too late.

✺ Chapter Thirteen ✺

She'd left too late. All she could see of the sun was a muted white glow above the trees. As soon as it dropped below the treetops, she'd be enclosed in darkness. In a snowstorm. Riding into the wind, she could feel the snow like needles against her face. She could, probably should, turn back. She could spend the night in the hotel. But Bette would be sick with worry. Maybe she could send a telegram. But she just wanted to get home, to sleep in her own bed. Sweet Pea knew the way. They'd be fine.

"You're doing good, girl." It helped to talk, to hear her voice out loud, even if the words were spoken through chattering teeth.

The muffled clomp of Sweet Pea's hooves suddenly changed. They sounded hollow. "The bridge. I know where we are." And where they were was far, far from home.

Her fingers were getting cold, so she alternated hands, putting one in her pocket while the other held the reins. She wiggled her toes inside her boots and pictured her room back at the hotel. Four-poster bed covered in a thick quilt. Hot coals in the fireplace giving the room a warm, red glow. Bette would be furious with her at first, but then she'd set a bed warmer to heat and fix her a cup of tea.

A tear slid down Lilly's cold cheek. There always seemed to be tension between her and Bette. As much as she wanted to blame her sister, she had to take much of the responsibility herself. From the day she'd arrived, she'd bristled against Bette's rules. But her sister was only trying to protect her and to keep her somewhat refined. As soon as she got home, she would tell her all of the things she was grateful for.

A gust of wind lifted her hat. Thankfully, the ties held it on. Her ears felt numb. This was dangerous. She'd gotten frostbite on two toes when she was fourteen and ignored the warning signs while skating with friends. Now, the tips of those toes burned, telling her all over again that she'd made a foolish mistake.

Movement caught her eye. The pendulum limb, swinging in the relentless wind. "That cabin. It was right near here." She slowed Sweet Pea and turned in the saddle. Had she passed it? *Lord, please, please, don't let me miss it.*

Holding the reins in one hand, she gripped the collar of her coat with the other. Every time Sweet Pea took a step, she whispered, "Please, please, please."

And then she saw it, alone on a rise, silhouetted against the pale pewter sky. She nudged Sweet Pea's neck. The horse turned off the road and picked up her pace, as if she sensed there was shelter ahead.

Lilly didn't try to slow her, despite the snow flying out from under her hooves in a cloud, making it even harder to see. When they reached the small, gray structure, it looked lonelier than it had at a distance.

"Hello?" she shouted before she dismounted. "Anyone home?" She held her breath, not wanting an answer. What kind of people lived in a place like this, in an unpainted, desolate shack with no curtains, no barn or shed, not even an outhouse? There was nothing scattered in front of the house. Not a rake or a bucket or a clothesline, and no sign that there'd ever been a garden.

When her greeting was met with silence, she slid off Sweet Pea's back and tied the reins to a post near the door. She patted the horse's damp mane. "I hate leaving you out in this."

She knocked on the door then tried the handle. The door swung open. In the last of the fading light, she spotted a lantern and a bundle of matches on a small table in front of a stone hearth. A pile of wood that should last the night sat next to a primitive rocking chair. "Thank You, Lord," she breathed.

She struck the match on the table, and it sputtered to life. The lantern globe was dusty, but the glow lit the room. The space was larger than it appeared from the outside. There was a loft above her. She could see the ends of two beds covered with patchwork quilts. Another bed, the small table, and a corner cupboard took up the end she stood in. About a third of the room was partitioned off with a half wall. She stepped closer. A pile of hay filled a wood feeding box. Straw covered the floor. Another door, this one on the side, was large enough for Sweet Pea.

Whoever owned this place shared it with their animals. Under any other circumstances, she would have found that fact distasteful. At the moment, it was the most welcome news she could have hoped for.

When she had Sweet Pea inside and unsaddled, she set about building a fire. The wood looked dry, but there was nothing small enough to be used as kindling. She searched the corner cupboard for a knife. Inside the single drawer she found three forks, three spoons, and a single sharp knife. And a Chicago and Northwestern train schedule.

A washbasin sat on top of the cupboard, and a towel hung from a hook on its side. Three ladder-back chairs were tucked under the table, a leather belt draped over one. And a rolled red bandanna.

Lilly tried to will away the chill. Lots of men used bandannas for handkerchiefs, or multiple other uses. She walked to the pile of wood, knelt, and set the knife on a split log. She took off her mittens and stuffed them in her pockets. As she picked up the knife again, a glint of dull metal caught her eye. There was something behind the stack of wood. Her hand shook as she picked it up. A hatchet. With *HB* stamped into the blade.

He had done some harebrained things in his life, but this might just top them all. If this was what love did to a person, he could understand why some of the loggers had sworn off women for life.

Élan adjusted the bandanna he'd tied over his face and pulled his fur-lined cap lower over his ears. Lollipop was walking now, slow and cautious. He gave the horse its head to pick her way through snow that was now six inches deep.

The one rational thing he'd done before leaving was to fill a saddlebag with items he might need. Bandages, a blanket, matches, a few sticks of dry wood, a full canteen, a change of clothes, and a piece of oilcloth he could use as a shelter if need be. He'd gone to the kitchen and wrapped a few biscuits in a cloth. The temperature had to be just below freezing. If he kept moving, he wouldn't freeze to death. Most likely, anyway.

As the evening wore on and the ridiculousness of what he was doing became more and more clear, he pictured Lilly's face when he found her, warm and safe and settled in for the night at the Mahl Hotel. How would he explain his actions? What would she say?

Would she see him as the fool he was, or would she finally understand how he felt about her?

Before he made any kind of move toward her, before he broke his promise to her sister, he needed to see something in Lilly's eyes that told him they were more than just friends.

As darkness closed in around him, he gave up scanning along the road...looking for what?

Did he really think she'd give up, stop, and wait for him? That he'd find her sitting atop her horse, covered in snow? In his rush to rescue the damsel, he'd discredited her. Though she could be a bit naive, she was also resourceful and quick-thinking. And most likely enjoying dinner at the hotel.

His stomach growled at the thought, and then another thought replaced it.

Maybe she hadn't eaten yet. He'd arrive at the hotel, get a room, wash up, change into clothes that didn't smell like he'd spent the morning working on machinery, and casually knock on her door. He'd say, "I read your note and thought I'd surprise you. Will you join me for dinner?" Then they'd walk into the dining room, her hand resting in the crook of his arm.

A break in the trees off in the distance revealed a flicker of light through a window on a low rise. He had to be getting close. But the road, now invisible, seemed to stretch on. Lollipop had instinctively kept to the middle of the open swath between the trees, and Élan prayed she wouldn't step off into a ditch or stumble in a hole.

And then, finally, another glimmer of light. A house, and then another. His whole body relaxed when he reached the hotel. Lilly would be inside, waiting for him.

He tethered Lollipop. He'd ask about Lilly then book a room and take his horse to the livery stable a block away.

The snow on his coat began to melt as soon as he walked in. He stepped over to the front desk, but before he could speak to the man behind it, someone called his name. A male voice.

William Pinkerton.

"Lamoreaux, what fortune!" Pinkerton walked toward him. "I hope my telegram didn't bring you out in this inclement weather."

"It did play a part. Any more information?"

"A few more details than I could share in my message to you. I think we're closing in, assuming they don't run." He nodded to an arched doorway behind him and to his right. "I was just about to go in for dinner. Join me."

"Thank you, I might. But I need to check on something first."

Élan turned around then stopped and looked back. "The woman you spoke to at camp, Lilly Galloway. Have you seen her here?"

"The rolling pin girl? Here? No."

The vision of escorting Lilly on his arm dissolved like the snow on his sleeves. "She left a note saying she was coming here this afternoon to talk to someone who knew Pascal."

"She came alone?"

Élan nodded, feeling the weight of guilt, as if he should have been keeping track of her every move, as if she were the kind of woman a man could hold in check. "I'll ask at the desk."

With Pinkerton close behind, he approached the man standing in front of the bank of cubbyholes for keys and messages. "I'm looking for a woman named Lilly Galloway. Can you tell me if she's staying here?"

The man glanced from him to Pinkerton. "She was here earlier, visiting Genevieve Duval, one of our permanent residents. She left. Maybe an hour and a half ago."

An hour and a half. Had she made it back to Embarrass before he'd even left the camp? He desperately wanted to believe that was so. But something in his gut told him otherwise. In good weather that would have been possible. Not in this. He turned to Pinkerton. "I have to find her."

A strong hand on his arm stopped him. "Not now. Not in this. I'll go with you at first light."

Élan's shoulders slumped. The man was right. There was nothing he could do now.

Nothing but talk to Genevieve Duval. And pray. And that he would do in earnest.

CHAPTER FOURTEEN

Staring at the hatchet in her hand, Lilly tried to make her brain work. Though it fit the description of the hatchet carried by one of the train robbers, wasn't it possible *HB* was a common maker's mark? For all she knew, the cabin might be owned by a sweet little old couple who'd just taken a train to visit their grandchildren.

But all the clues put together...rolled red bandanna, train schedule, *HB* on the hatchet...it was hard to make any other conclusion stick.

Should she start a fire? No sane person would be out in this storm, but if the wind died down by morning, someone might spot the chimney smoke. If her suspicions were right, and she'd somehow found herself in the train robbers' hideout, what would they do if they found her here? Would they barge in with guns blazing?

If it was Axe and Jimmie, they wouldn't hurt her. Would they? Then again, if her suspicions were right, they weren't the men she thought they were. Their joking about becoming kidnappers and train robbers hadn't been joking at all. It was hard to reconcile the two pictures...the men who teased her on Sunday mornings and played music for the camp church services didn't seem capable of holding up a train.

Even though they had always treated her kindly, if they found her here they might turn on her like cornered animals. She remembered a gruesome story one of the older loggers had told her about a lion trainer somewhere in England who had slipped and fallen during a show. In seconds, four lions were on top of him, mauling him to death.

She closed her eyes and set the hatchet down. She could survive the night without a fire. But that was ridiculous. If the men showed up, they would come in, fire or not. She might as well stay warm, and at first light she and Sweet Pea would be on the road, headed home. Picking up the axe again, she shaved thin strips of wood until she had a pile of curlicues, and then, despite feeling weak all over, managed to get a good fire going.

Her stomach growled. "Wonder if they left anything to eat." Sweet Pea turned her head at Lilly's voice, contentedly munching on hay without a care in the world. Lilly stood and brushed off her coat. She picked up the lantern and opened the top door of the corner cupboard. Three shelves. On the bottom shelf were plates, bowls, and enamel cups. Three of each. On the middle shelf she found a can of tomato soup, a tin of soda crackers, a box of cream of wheat, and a jar of tea. Supper and breakfast. "Thank You, Lord." Could His provision have been more perfect?

The top shelf held a metal pot. And a book. She pulled the book toward her and felt her knees go weak. *The Art of Cooking French* by Jean-Claude Pascal.

Three place settings. For Axe, Jimmie…and Jean-Claude?

Heart heavy, she picked up the pot and walked out into an angry wind, gulping air as she filled the pot with snow. "'The Lord is on my side; I will not fear: what can man do unto me?'" She recited the verse from Psalm 118 out loud, once, and then again, as if she addressed whatever evil might be slinking around in the darkness.

By the time she'd hung the pot of snow on a hook over the fire, the room had warmed enough that she could remove her coat. When she'd heated the soup, she sat at the little table and thanked God, again for His provision. She was warm and dry, with a meal spread before her. The storm that had forced her to seek shelter here was now protecting her.

With each bite, she felt her strength return and her mind clear. It dawned on her what she'd done. She'd found the train robbers' lair. But there was no triumph in it. She would have to telegraph Mr. Pinkerton. But instead of rejoicing that she'd been the one to lead him to the criminals, she felt like she was betraying dear friends.

Why hadn't it occurred to her until right now that this was the reason Pinkerton was at the camp? He was searching for the men who had held up the train. Had Jean-Claude willingly colluded, or had they abducted him, hoping for the reward, or a ransom? Had there been a ransom note? Had Élan kept that information from her along with his suspicions about Axe and Jimmie?

Looking around the little cabin, she wondered who had built it. It had to be older than Axe, and he was at least fifty. Was it a young couple, just starting out? Or a trapper who traded with the natives when this was a vast untamed wilderness? Maybe it was built by the famous French explorer Jean Nicolet.

Why did Axe and Jimmie need a hideout? They were part of the small crew that lived at the camp year-round. When did they use this place? If they were away from camp for stretches at a time, what was their explanation? Why not just use Soleil Rouge as their base?

Because they'd need a place to hide their take.

That had to be it. Which meant the money from the latest robbery could be right here. Right under her feet, or over her head, or in the walls.

Lilly set down her spoon and stood. "Sweet Pea, we're on a mission. If that money is here, we are going to find it before first light."

Every muscle in Élan's tired body ached. From the ride, the tension, and from fighting with a flat pillow on a too-soft mattress all night…a night haunted by images of Lilly huddling under pine branches, trying to stay warm. Would she have known enough to get up and move to keep her blood circulating, to not fall asleep? Falling asleep in the cold could mean…

Having slept in his clothes, there was no need to change. He'd keep the clean shirt and pants in his pack in case Lilly needed them, or if he needed something to wrap her cold, still—

"Stop it!" He yelled at the image in the mirror above the washbasin. "She's alive. I know it." Wouldn't he feel it, deep in his soul, if she wasn't?

Lilly was resourceful. Maybe she'd even brought matches. He shook his head. She wouldn't have thought of that, not when she'd only planned on being gone for a few hours. Wherever she was, had Sweet Pea stayed with her, or found her way back to camp? A riderless horse would cause alarm. Maybe the men were, even now, saddling up to form a search party.

He picked up his watch for the tenth time since he'd crawled out of the torturous bed. The sun would be up in half an hour. He grabbed his coat and pack and headed down the stairs.

William Pinkerton was already in the dining room, talking to a woman with silver hair and a flouncy gown that seemed a bit too fancy for this time of the morning. When he walked over to them, Pinkerton introduced them. Genevieve Duvall. Jean-Claude's grandmother. She had already retired for the evening when they'd wanted to speak to her last night. Now she held out a thin, blue-veined hand. "I have heard so much about you, Mr. Lamoreaux, and I met your beautiful Lilly yesterday."

"Sh-she is not…mine."

A knowing smile crinkled the pale skin around her eyes. "Not yet. My Jean-Claude has a Frenchman's intuition. He knows true love when he sees it." She winked at him. "My advice to you is do not hesitate. Let the Lord guide you."

"I…will." He flushed under Pinkerton's curious gaze.

"I understand you are in a hurry. As I told the detective, Lilly was wearing a heavy wool coat when she left, and she seemed to be a very bright young woman." Her smile faded and her eyes glistened as if she was about to cry. "As to my grandson…I pray you will go easy on him."

"Easy? What do you know about his whereabouts?"

"Nothing. But I fear he may have returned to some of his old ways. I have medical concerns, and I know he feels responsible to help." She opened a small handbag covered in sequins. "When I read the description of the men who robbed the train, I couldn't help but think of this." She pulled out a photograph.

Axe and Jimmie stood, each with an arm around the shoulders of the short man in the middle.

A tear slid down Genevieve's lined cheek. "He calls these two men his best friends."

As Élan rode out of town next to Pinkerton, the sun rose on a scene that would have been stunningly beautiful under other circumstances. Sugared branches glistened. The ground sparkled with diamonds. A hush fell over the world. But Élan's gaze was not on the beauty around him as he scanned both sides of the road, looking for anything that seemed abnormal.

They stopped at the first farmhouse outside of town, but no one, of course, had seen a young woman on horseback in the middle of a blizzard.

Élan also stopped twice to brush snow off a lump in the grass. Just a log and a hay bale, thank the Lord. His breathing was shallow, his pulse fast, as they came upon another body-sized hump in the snow.

Pinkerton held up a hand, slowed his horse, and slid down. "Stay where you are. I'll check this."

Élan told himself not to look but couldn't obey his own orders. Pinkerton nudged something with his foot then bent to brush off snow. Something red. Élan held his breath.

"It's a cushion. From a carriage seat, I'd guess."

Air whooshed from his lungs, and he prodded Lollipop to keep going. Another mile, and he spotted something. A trail in the snow. Maybe just a deer path, but something or someone had walked here, kicking up snow. An inch or so had fallen on top of it, but the way was still visible. He held up his hand, and Pinkerton stopped too.

"Leads up to that cabin."

"I see smoke. Pretty sure I saw light from inside last night."

Pinkerton pulled his gun out of its saddle ring. "I'll go first."

The gun didn't seem necessary at this point. They were probably going to be waking an elderly hermit, but he supposed it was something Pinkerton was trained to do. Or maybe it was a case of overactive nerves. Élan patted Lollipop's neck as they moved almost soundlessly up the path. They dismounted at the top of the rise and tethered the horses to a branch. Élan holstered his gun and prayed he wouldn't have to use it.

"Around back," Pinkerton whispered.

Élan wanted to ask why they couldn't just walk up to the front door and knock, but it wasn't his place to question. Maybe they were checking for a back door and one of them would guard it while the other went to the front.

They walked around the corner of the cabin. "There," Élan whispered, pointing. Next to the lone tree behind the cabin, a pile of fresh dirt was mounded on top of the snow. A small hole, most likely. Not large enough to be a grave. Unless someone had only started…

The single window in the rear was too high to look in. Pinkerton pressed close to the wall and slunk around the next corner then jumped back as a door was flung open.

Pinkerton aimed his gun. And a woman screamed.

Sweet Pea reared at her scream, slamming her against the doorframe. She held tight to the reins as the horse bolted out the open door. Lilly's feet slid out from under her, and she landed on the stone walkway, banging her head. Stars swam in front of her eyes. She released the reins. And the world went black.

"…hit her head…doctor…to Shawano…back to camp…keep her here…" Fragments of a conversation drifted into moments of consciousness along with sparks of light. They'd lit the fire again. But she'd just put it out. Were they making her stay? Was Élan only in her imagination? She'd only gotten a glimpse of the two men, one with a gun pointed at her. Maybe she'd willed one of them to be him. Maybe it was really Axe and Jimmie. Then where was Jean-Claude? Tears stung her eyes as she thought of Genevieve. She would be crushed to discover her Jean-Claude was on his way to prison.

"Thunderation!" The shout brought her back to consciousness. "Look what was tied to her saddle!" The exclamation, in a voice she recognized as William Pinkerton's, was followed by a sound she knew.

Bags of coins slamming onto the table.

"Lamoreaux, that crazy rolling-pin girl of yours found the payroll money. Think maybe I'll have to hire her."

∽ CHAPTER FIFTEEN ∾

Élan paced the tiny room that had been Jean-Claude's, alternating between praying out loud and whispering, "Wake up so I can tell you I love you," under his breath.

Three days. Lilly had been unconscious for three days. Pinkerton had left him at the cabin with her and ridden hard back to camp to send men with a wagon for Lilly, then he'd ridden into Embarrass to fetch the doctor. By the time they were on their way, it was getting dark, so they'd come to the camp, and the doctor said she couldn't be moved again.

Dr. Martin had come every day. Bette, Dottie, and Evening Star had taken turns tending her. Élan felt useless, to Lilly and to the camp, unable to do anything but pace and pray.

Cutting had started at the new site. He should be there, but Slim had surprised him by stepping up and taking charge. Though he didn't talk much, when he did, the men listened, and he'd shown an uncanny ability to manage schedules and handle ordering supplies.

Slim had hooked up the wanigan this morning and left with the rest of the crew. This was what his mother would call a blessing in disguise. The camp was in good hands. Maybe this was a sign.

"Mr. Lamoreaux?"

Evening Star stood in the doorway. "Mr. Pinkerton would like to see you. And Lilly."

"Send him in."

William Pinkerton, who'd arrived at Soleil Rouge less than a week ago looking pressed and clean and dignified, now looked like a fur trapper in a dirty suede jacket, fur cap, and a three-day beard. "How's she doing?"

Élan shrugged. "Doc thinks she'll wake up soon."

"Good. I still can't believe just seeing that shovel leaning against a tree would make her think to dig under it. Wish I could be here to see her face when she gets the money."

"Money?"

A grin like Élan had never seen on the man split his face. "Reward money. We got 'em. We set up a stakeout in the woods, and they finally returned right after sunup this morning."

Élan was afraid to ask. Pinkerton had interrogated Axe and Jimmie for hours on Saturday but hadn't learned a thing. They claimed to have gone to a dance over in Marion that Friday night and hadn't come back to camp until morning. They both vowed they knew nothing about the train robbery or what happened to Jean-Claude. He braced himself with a hand on the chair next to the cot. "Are they my men?"

"Nope. I'll admit I didn't believe their alibis at first, but they checked out."

Élan let out a long-held breath.

"The real robbers are three guys from Minnesota."

"Three?"

Pinkerton nodded. "The old one confessed to the two train robberies here and a couple in Iowa and implicated the other two. Apparently the third man is the brains behind their heists. He makes the plans, and the other two carry them out. Pretty sure they're all going to be behind bars for a long, long time."

Élan sat with a thud. Axe and Jimmie were innocent. "Any connection to Jean-Claude?"

"Actually, yes." Pinkerton laughed. "The skinny one got very talkative when I told him honesty would play in his favor. Apparently, he started his life of crime by stealing luggage on the docks in Green Bay. There was a cookbook in one, written by a man named Jean-Claude Pascal."

Stunned silence was Élan's only response, and then he shook his head and laughed. "Small world, as they say. I may not have hired the little Frenchmen if he hadn't been flat broke."

Pinkerton pulled an envelope out of his pocket and handed it to Élan. "There's enough here for Lilly to be sittin' pretty for a long time to come."

Sittin' pretty. That meant she'd have enough money to pay off her sister's debt and move back to Milwaukee. It also meant she might not be open to what he was going to offer. Élan thanked Pinkerton and congratulated him on closing the case. And then he stood. And started pacing and praying all over again.

Lilly woke to the sound of dishes clattering and the smell of side pork frying. And something else. Fennel. And orange. Where was she? Slowly, she opened one eye. As light from the east window streamed in, so did awareness. She was still at Soleil Rouge, still in Jean-Claude's little room behind the kitchen. Thanks to a very understanding doctor, she'd stayed several days longer than she needed to. A spot on the back of her head ached a bit, and her elbow hurt when she straightened it, but other than that, she was good as new. If she kept up the charade any longer, Bette would become suspicious.

As she got out of bed and began getting dressed, snippets of mostly one-sided conversations began reassembling like pieces of a crazy quilt. The robbers were behind bars. There'd been some kind of reward. Élan had given it to Bette for safekeeping. Axe and Jimmie were not guilty, and they thought it very funny that she had suspected them. They were friends with Jean-Claude but had no idea why he'd left.

Élan had received a response to a letter he'd written to the Palmer House. Jean-Claude had not accepted their offer of a position in their kitchen, under any name. Pinkerton had gone back to Chicago. He was not looking for Jean-Claude. No one was looking for him. She'd wasted precious time by tripping over her own two feet.

As she ran a brush through her hair, a knock at the door warmed her cheeks. She recognized the rhythm. Her Moose. "Come in."

He opened the door and stepped inside. "Good morning. Ready to go home?"

No. The past week, since she'd regained consciousness, had been wonderful. Though she'd hated the role of invalid, she hadn't minded one bit having Élan sitting beside her, holding her hand and whispering words he thought she couldn't hear. What she didn't know was whether, in a state of half-consciousness, she'd answered him.

Once she'd been able to get out of bed and walk, the doctor had ordered her to be up and moving for short periods of time, so she'd spent that time in the kitchen, supervising meal preparations and teaching Evening Star the art of pie baking. In just a few days, Evening Star, George, Henry, and Tobias were working as efficiently as that hay baler she'd seen at the fair. Élan himself had said she was working her way out of a job.

She started to nod in answer to Élan's question then changed her mind. "Actually, I'm not ready to go home. I rather like the role of princess, being waited on hand and foot. I think I'd like to stay on in that capacity."

He laughed. "I suppose that could be arranged." His smile flattened. "I guess you'll be wanting to return to a life of leisure now."

"Life of leisure? Is that how you see my job at the hotel?" She swirled her hair into a bun, not easy with her stiff elbow.

"No. I mean…you'll be going back to Milwaukee."

What was he talking about? "Why would I want to do that?"

"Because of the reward money."

She picked up a tortoiseshell comb. "How much was it?"

"You don't know?"

"No. Bette took it. I was hoping maybe I could get a new dress for Christmas with it."

Élan's laughter filled the little room. "You can buy yourself a whole catalog's worth of dresses for two thousand dollars."

"Two—" The comb slipped from her hand and bounced under the cot. Lilly dropped to her knees just as Élan did the same. Their eyes locked. Was he remembering kneeling in the wet snow right after she'd accused him of murdering Jean-Claude, right before she was sure he was going to kiss her? The same look softened his features now.

The clang of something dropped in the next room brought her back to the moment. She felt beneath the cot until her hand met something. Not a comb. This was soft. She drew it out. An empty money pouch, about the size of her hand. Brown leather, with something burned into it. She moved to position it in the sunlight, so she could make it out. Two *R*s, back-to-back. "I've seen this brand somewhere." Why did it look familiar?

"Ross Reynolds." Élan hissed the name. "He's a bounty hunter. Lives somewhere near Tomahawk."

"Bounty? So he was after the reward money offered by the Savoy?"

"Had to be."

What had the reward notice said? Captured dead or alive? Her stomach clenched, but as she stared at the brand, the feeling she'd seen it somewhere became stronger. "Red River!"

"The town? Or the river? Or…"

"A couple of years ago, we got a reservation by mail from the Red River Logging Camp. This symbol was on the letterhead."

Élan's fists clenched. "They bribed him."

Lilly sighed. "You still don't believe me. He would never have left Auguste."

Élan held out his hand for the pouch. "It's empty."

"That doesn't mean…" She couldn't finish the statement. At the moment, her brain still numb from what Élan had just told her about the reward money, she wasn't sure of anything. For all she knew, the pouch may have belonged to one of the train robbers from Minnesota. Maybe they'd threatened to turn Jean-Claude in if he didn't help them. Or maybe they'd simply paid him to help. As far as she knew, the question of why there was three of everything in their hideaway hadn't yet been answered.

"I don't know what it means, but because you seem to have a knack for solving crimes, I will go and check it out. I'll leave on Sunday morning when they'll all be in camp."

"Not without me, you won't."

"You are in no condition to—"

"Excuse me, sir. I am a legal adult, two days from my twenty-third birthday. I am capable of making my own decisions. And I have decided I am going with you."

CHAPTER SIXTEEN

"Then we are in agreement?" Élan tucked the folded papers into his shirt pocket and held his hand out to Lilly's sister.

Bette took his hand and shook it, a hint of a smile touching her usually sad eyes. "We have an agreement."

"Will you tell her I'm here?"

"I will." The smile broadened just before she turned, skirts swishing, and headed for the stairs.

He could read her thoughts. Bette was sure she knew her sister's mind better than he did. Élan prayed that wasn't true. He paced the foyer for a moment then suddenly stopped and walked into a room he'd only seen from the doorway. The parlor was reserved for registered hotel guests. The decor was so different than the dark, somber Mahl Hotel. This room felt cheery, yet calming, a place where a person could feel at home away from home. He left the parlor and walked into the kitchen, startling Dottie.

"The elder Miss Galloway's goin' to have your handsome head on a platter, Mr. Lamoreaux." Dottie wiped her hands on her apron and walked toward him, raising short, plump arms to embrace him.

"Let her try." He grinned. "Anything you need me to sample?"

Dottie nodded to a pan of biscuits. "See if those will pass muster."

He slathered the still warm biscuit with butter and strawberry jam and had just taken a bite when Lilly walked in, a leather bag slung over her shoulder, followed by Bette. He greeted Lilly with a hearty "Good morning!" and aimed a too-sweet smile at Bette.

Lilly looked from him to Bette, clearly expecting her to give him a tongue lashing for daring to set foot in the kitchen. When Bette merely smiled stiffly, Lilly's brow furrowed.

"Here," Dottie intervened. "I've packed a few sandwiches, some cookies, and a jar of coffee for yer journey, and I'll be prayin' every second you're away."

"Thank you," Élan said. "We will keep her safe. The rest of the men are meeting us about a mile from the camp. The Red River men will be sleeping off their Saturday night revelry, and we'll catch them off guard." With that, they said their goodbyes and walked out.

Two horses stood saddled and ready. "What's that French word for when you feel like you've done the exact same thing before?" she asked.

"*Déjà vu*." He laced his hands for her to step into.

"That's it." This time she accepted his offer of a boost into the saddle. "Was it just two weeks ago we rode off like this and I told you how I longed for adventure?"

Élan nudged Lollipop, and they headed left on Main Street. "Have you had more than you hoped for?"

"No. Never. Maybe enough danger for a while, but not too much adventure. You know, I overheard what Mr. Pinkerton said about offering me a job."

Élan's face reddened. He turned to her then quickly averted his eyes. "You…were awake?"

"Off and on."

"What else…did you hear?"

She paused a moment, thinking of all the delicious ways she could answer. Every one of them would embarrass him. "Nothing I wasn't happy to hear."

His lips parted then curved in a shy smile. His foot tapped Lollipop's side, and they picked up speed as they left town, cantering as they passed the last house then breaking into a gallop. The wind in her face was exhilarating.

Élan slowed their pace, and they rode in silence for an hour. As the sun rose in a sky the color of Élan's eyes, Lilly lifted her face, savoring a bit of warmth they hadn't felt in days. Tiny sparks glittered in the snow. They had no idea what they would encounter when they reached the Red River camp, but it was hard to imagine anything bad happening on a day this pristine.

After they passed Soleil Rouge, the snow on the road was churned up from hooves and footsteps and wagon wheel tracks. "How many of the men are meeting us?"

"All of them."

Lilly pulled back on the reins, and Sweet Pea came to a stop. "*All* of them? What if I'm wrong? What if Jean-Claude isn't there, or he's working for them willingly?"

Élan slowed Lollipop and turned in the saddle, pressing a hand to his chest. "Your doubt hurts me to the core. You must believe me, Papillon, he would not have left his precious Auguste behind. It is his most prized possession in all the world, a symbol of what his life once was and who he could have become if he had not been wrongly accused of—" His comical rendition of her tirade came to a sudden halt when she pressed her legs into Sweet Pea's sides and flew past him.

When he caught up with her, his eyes sparkled with pure delight. "All right. Slow down, and I will tell you the truth. I sent Axe and Jimmie out on a reconnaissance mission last night. They met a couple of the Red River men at a tavern and found out the truth. They admitted that Jean-Claude was kidnapped so he would cook for them. They said he put up a good fight but was overpowered. They did not know what is being done to keep him there."

"And you are just telling me this now? They could be torturing him, locking him in shackles every night. Or threatening his grandmother! That would explain why he hasn't dared let anyone know where he is." She thought of a novel she'd been unable to finish reading. "The camp is owned by a Frenchman, isn't it? I read about what Napoleon's men did to prisoners. Thumbscrews and a rack that stretched their bodies until—" She could not put the gruesome facts into words.

An amused smile appeared. One with which she was all too familiar. "They would not harm him bodily, *mon cherie*. They need him healthy so he can feed them coq au vin and crêpes suzette. But I am sure he is in emotional distress, and I am ashamed that I did not believe you from the beginning. If I had, I could have sent men to Red River and some of the other camps. I confess I have never believed Jean-Claude's story of his innocence, and I thought it most likely he had simply moved on for more money, or the law had finally caught up with him." He gave a sheepish look. "Can you forgive me, Papillon?"

His sad puppy dog face made it impossible to stay mad. "I forgive you." She lifted her chin and arched one eyebrow. "When I am a Pinkerton agent, will you start believing me?"

"Yes, Detective Butterfly, then you will have my full respect."

A few moments later, they met up with the Soleil Rouge men. Most on foot, a few on horseback. All appearing to be having the time of their lives. The group parted like the Red Sea, allowing Élan and Lilly to move to the front.

Lilly pictured what might happen when they entered the camp en masse. "What if the Red River men think we're here to attack them and they start shooting?"

"We have a plan for that. George, Henry, you lead the charge."

"Charge?" Her voice quaked.

George and Henry stepped in front of them. And began to sing. "Allons enfants de la Patrie. Le jour de gloire est arrivé…" Other voices, Élan's the loudest, joined in a rowdy chorus of "La Marseillaise."

The sight and sounds that greeted them when they walked into an open area in the middle of the camp caused the song to fade into the cold air.

Jean-Claude sat in a chair beside a roaring campfire with his stocking feet propped on a stump. A buffalo robe covered his lap. Two men played fiddles, and another sat on a low stool, polishing Jean-Claude's boots. Another held out a tray sporting a china cup, teapot, and a plate of macarons.

With a satisfied grin on his face, Jean-Claude held up one hand, stopping the music. "Ah. Finally, Lamoreaux. I knew you would come to my rescue. I suppose you would like me to return. Shall we discuss terms?"

Lilly sat on a hard, rough bench next to Evening Star on Sunday afternoon. She was surprised to see more than half of the men in attendance, a few with wives, one with two young children. Jean-Claude was not present. As usual, he spent this time with his Mamie.

Two weeks ago, she'd lumped these men all together, calling them "heathen louts." Now, waiting for the service to begin, she repented for not seeing them as individuals with hopes and dreams and family connections...with lives apart from the camp, at least for a few months out of the year.

A verse from the Book of Proverbs her father had often quoted came to mind. *He that answereth a matter before he heareth it, it is folly and shame unto him.* Élan got up from his seat and stood in front. Before he said a word, a hush fell over the room, and Lilly felt the same sense of awe she'd had when the dining room was empty. The men bowed their heads, and Élan began to pray.

As she listened to the reverence in his voice, she wondered what his father would think of him now. And then a second thought made her throat tighten. *This is where he belongs.* Not necessarily here, at Soleil Rouge, but in this role, inviting others to draw closer to God. Did he know that?

After the amen, Élan sat, and the man they called Winnipeg, bent and weathered from years as a logger, stepped to the front of the room with Axe. Jimmie and Cordwood, a man about Lilly's age who reminded her of a scrawny sapling, joined them. The room filled with the sweet, clear strains of "Tell Me the Stories of Jesus" then swept into "Blessed Assurance." Tears filled Lilly's eyes. As she looked around the room, she realized she was not the only one affected so deeply. She'd sung these songs her whole life, but never had the words reached deep into her soul like this. As they sang the "wretch like me" verse at the beginning of "Amazing Grace," she felt a kinship with these roughhewn men that she couldn't explain.

Élan stood. "Today's reading is from the seventh chapter of the book of Matthew." As he read and then began to expound on the passage that spoke of taking the beam out your own eye before pointing out the mote in someone else's, she experienced a strange mingling of deep conviction and pride. Her Moose had the gift of teaching.

When the service ended, she buttoned up her coat but waited in her seat until the room emptied. Élan picked up a well-worn Bible and walked toward her. "You're looking very serious for your birthday, Papillon."

"I need to say something to you, and I'm not sure how you will take it."

The peace she'd seen on his face in the past hour seemed to shatter at her words. "I have been expecting this." He dropped onto the bench next to her.

"You have?"

He nodded. "Since the reward money. I don't blame you."

"Blame me? For what?"

"For wanting to go back to the city where life is more exciting."

He'd said that yesterday. Hadn't she set him straight? No, she'd dropped her comb and hadn't answered him. "My dear sweet Moose..." It slipped out before she had a chance to "take every thought captive." "I have no intention of leaving. I love it here. Yes, I do want adventures and excitement, but not the kind I'd find in Milwaukee. I love the forest and the animals and baking, and I want to take more time to get to know our guests and the loggers and figure out why God put me here and what more He wants me to be doing. What I need to tell you is that you need to go back to seminary. Or not. Maybe you can learn everything you need to know right here, but however you do it, I believe with my whole heart that God has called you to be a preacher."

Was there a word in Webster's English Dictionary for this look of shock, relief, and joy all rolled into one? Élan jumped to his feet and grabbed her hand. "Come with me."

She scrambled to keep up with his long strides as he led her out the door and along the snowy path to his cabin. He opened the front door and motioned for her to step in front of him.

This space she'd longed to see was in every way more than she had imagined. Rocking chair by the stone fireplace. A patchwork quilt in blues and greens covered a bed made from intertwined curved branches that made her think of her tree house back in Milwaukee. She wanted to inspect every corner, but Élan stood next to something about her height, covered in another quilt. She knew instantly what it was.

"I had intended this to be a surprise, but I'm beginning to realize it's not easy to stay a step ahead of you."

"Especially when my steps lead me to tripping over the surprise."

He laughed and pointed to the rocking chair. She sat, and he pulled a sheaf of folded papers out of his pocket and knelt in front of her. "The Lord has been telling me exactly what you just told me. I don't know how that will all work out, but I found out last week that Slim is perfectly capable of taking over as foreman. If Greeley approves, I will start training him immediately, because I'll soon have my hands full with my new venture."

"What's that?"

"As of yesterday morning"—he waved the papers—"I am a hotelier."

"A hotel—" Her eyes felt like they were going to pop out of her head. "Y-you bought the Galloway?"

"Yes. But since you're now in a position to pay it off yourself, I need to give you the option—"

She stopped him with a shake of her head. "No options. Go on." She could barely hear her words over the pounding in her ears.

"Well"—he took her hand in his—"I was wondering if maybe you'd like to go into partnership with me."

Partnership? That was what he had in mind? And here she thought he was on the verge of proposing. *Can he still be so blind that he doesn't—*

"For better or worse."

"For…what?" she whispered.

"For life. Forever. I love you. I have loved you since you were a sixteen-year-old giggly girl in braids. Will you marry me, Papillon?"

Tears practically leapt over her bottom lashes, spilling onto his hand. "Yes. Of course, yes."

He reached out and took her into his arms then pressed his lips to hers until she felt she floated in an azure summer sky. Then he pulled away and stood abruptly. "I want to propose something else." He helped her to her feet. "I think that, since you will no longer be a Galloway, and no one can pronounce my name, we should change the name of the hotel." He pinched a corner of the cloth covering the thing that stood in the middle of the room and yanked it away.

A moose, carved from a tree stump, now fully formed, with a butterfly perched on its nose. The moose's eyes were crossed. The butterfly's were bright green.

Lilly stepped forward and touched one of the butterfly eyes.

"It's bottle glass. Jean-Claude's suggestion. What do you think about changing the name of the hotel to the 'Moose and Butterfly Inn'?"

She stared up into sky-blue eyes. "I love it. The moose, and the butterfly, and the name." She placed one hand on an antler and the other on the whiskered cheek of her Moose, and then she kissed him. "And I love you. For better, for worse, and forever."

An Embarrassment of Riches

by

Cynthia Ruchti

"For whoever wants to save their life will lose it,

but whoever loses their life for me will find it."

—MATTHEW 16:25 (NIV)

∽ Chapter One ∽

Embarrass, Wisconsin

Present Day

"Did you know you can make mango ice cream with only two ingredients?"

Elliott Lansing switched to speakerphone so he could pull back onto the highway. "Piper, as always, you're a fountain of fascinating information, but I need an answer, if you don't mind."

"Three ingredients, if you count the splash of vanilla. A frozen banana, frozen mango, blend, and ta-da! Mango ice cream."

If he hadn't had both hands on the wheel like his grandma taught him, he would have rubbed his eyebrows off. "Piper?"

"It's relevant to your problem. Picture this. Sorbet tastings at eight every evening when the inn is full of guests. Or a guest. One guest would be enough. Mango, raspberry, lemon."

Piper's voice seemed even more vibrant as it bounced around the interior of Elliott's car. No one could accuse the woman of lacking a zest for life. But it wasn't her zest he needed right now. He was desperate for her marketing acumen.

"Ooh," she said, "maybe switch out one flavor for strawberry. Do they have pick-your-own strawberry patches around here, or is that yet another…embarrassment?"

Ah, a breath. "Piper, I've always appreciated your sense of humor."

"Always?"

"Most of the time. I'd love to tell my grandmother she doesn't have to worry about her financial future after she retires from inn-keeping. But I can't in good conscience say that."

"Yet."

"Of all people, you know that a place like hers, in a small town with a name like Embarrass, is not likely to draw top dollar even if she *could* sell it. She's in big trouble, Piper. And rather than possessing the marketing genius of someone like you, I—as they say—have a face for radio."

"All our college friends who didn't already have a boyfriend would beg to differ."

"Piper…"

"Your face is just fine."

"Fine?"

"More than fine. It's…adequate. It's your voice that could melt a glacier."

"Nice one. And it's my job. That's what I bring to the table. Voice acting. Not sure it's the skillset Gram needs from me right now."

"Melting chocolate?"

Elliott sighed.

"Convince tourists to flock to a non-touristy town and stay in an aging, lackluster inn?"

"If that's your sales pitch ability…"

The background noise coming through the phone sounded familiar.

"Elliott, my friend, I have a plane to catch. Can we finish this conversation later?"

"A plane to catch? Where to?" That was *all* he needed right now. She'd be lounging on a beach in Mexico while he tried to keep his grandmother from having to file bankruptcy.

"A little place called Ashwaubenon. Near Green Bay. You might have heard of it."

"That's our closest airport. You decided to accept the offer?"

"You offered me half what I usually make."

"And all the cheese curds you can eat."

Her laughter was irresistible. "I'm not accepting *your* offer. I'm cutting it by half again. Call it a ten-year post-graduation itch for a challenge. This one's just too delicious. Which brings us back to mango ice cream."

"Or sorbet."

"Exactly. I'm reeling with ideas."

"Not unexpected."

A gate announcement in the background let Elliott know she was indeed serious.

"Did you expect I would turn you down?" she asked.

"Hoped you wouldn't. Thought you would."

"We should have kept in touch better after college. You don't know me very well. The new me. I've come out of my shell."

"Heaven help us all."

"They just called first class. Gotta go. I'll see you a few hours from now."

"First class? Nice."

"I'm kidding. Getting ready to settle into a lovely middle seat in steerage."

"What time do you land? I'll pick you up at the airport."

"Negatory. I'm renting a car. I'll need my own wheels for the investigation stage. Meet you in Embarrassment."

"It's Embarrass, Piper."

"Got it."

Grandma Peggy, you didn't do yourself any favors keeping a has-been inn in a town with a name that means shame.

"I prefer the French definition, Elliott."

Elliott tugged his grandmother's two-ton suitcase down the sidewalk to the curb where her ride waited.

"*Stuck?* That definition of *Riviere Embarrasser*?"

"You know the French, Son. It's a little more romantic than 'stuck.'"

"Log jam?"

"Closer. I've always believed this little inn of mine is a gem right here in the heart of Embarrass, Wisconsin. An embarrassment of riches, if you will."

"The heart of Embarrass is pretty close to its liver and gall bladder, Gram."

"Elliott!"

"I just mean, towns don't get much smaller than this." He hoisted her luggage into the back of the Honda. "*Oof!* I hope you're prepared to pay extra for this bag, Grandma."

"My friend Evelyn is even covering that cost too. How did I get so blessed? A month in Europe, all expenses paid, including my flight, my overweight luggage, and ruckus-canceling headphones she bought to help me sleep on the trans-Atlantic flight."

"Noise-canceling."

"What? Oh, yes. And a grandson with a heart of gold. I'm grateful for you, Elliott." She stood on tiptoe to plant a kiss on his cheek. "I realize the enormity of the task you're taking on. I'll hold nothing against you if this scheme of yours doesn't work out. I've known for a long time that I couldn't count on the sale of the inn to fund my retirement dreams. I will simply become one of those people whose status is 'fixed income' and who clips coupons to buy ramen noodles."

"I won't let that happen." *Can't let that happen.* "I hope Evelyn plans to be the one to hoist this bag for you during your trip."

"Nonsense. She's in her eighties."

"Gram?"

"But fairly fit for her age. Oh, don't worry. I packed another piece of luggage inside that one. I'll divide the weight between the two of them once we arrive on the Continent, as they say."

"That's what you're hauling to Europe? An extra suitcase?"

"And a heart that desperately needs to immerse itself in some history, beauty, architecture, culture, and at least one dream fulfilled before I toddle off to the Home." She lifted her chin. "Evelyn and I will miss April in Paris, but I hear May's nice too."

He bent for one last hug and kissed the cheek that was far softer than his. "I love you. Please take care of yourself. And keep in touch."

"As able. I have a lot of living to pack into this next month."

Elliott watched her climb into the car. *She didn't mean that to sound ominous or foreboding, did she?*

Elliott heard a car door slam out front. Seconds later, his phone pinged with a text from Piper.

Here.

He closed his laptop on the marble-topped desk in the smallest second-floor guest room he'd chosen for his recording studio. Its sound-dampening position at the rear of the house under the never-used narrow attic stairway would have to do.

Tempted to say "Coming!" aloud as he padded through the empty halls, he resisted and took a moment to peer through the front-facing window at the sidewalk below.

Piper stood on the sidewalk as a child might, head tilted back to take in the scope of the building. Rather, as a child might when anticipating the terrifying first day in an unfamiliar school...in a bad neighborhood...already regretting the move.

Her mouth hung open, eyes wide, eyebrows arched, looking but not moving her head. Smileless and guileless, but definitely overwhelmed.

Elliott was pretty sure it wasn't because of the inn's grandeur. That had long faded.

He tapped on the window and caught her attention. Only then did her face erupt in a broad smile. She waved as if the kindergartner inside her had just caught a glimpse of someone blessedly familiar at her new school.

Piper Merrill leaned into their welcome hug as long as she dared. He looked good. More than she could say for the inn. Did they not think a coat of paint a dozen years ago might have helped? Or a sign out front with words the sun hadn't bleached paler than nude lipstick? If it hadn't been for her navigation system, she might not have found the place.

Elliott released his hold on her and reached for her leopard-print luggage—both pieces. "Safe flight?"

"Emotionally or physically?"

"What?"

"No turbulence. Had the whole row of two seats to myself. But when I checked in, I was asked, as always, 'Final destination?'"

"Ashwaubenon. That likely raised a few eyebrows."

"Would have. But that's not where my mind was. I said, 'Embarrass. I'm heading for Embarrass.'"

Elliott chuckled, his laugh as rich and deep as his narration voice.

"It felt like I was telling the world I'm from Frog Spit, Arkansas." Piper scanned her surroundings. "But that would be warmer than here."

"You should visit this place in winter. By comparison, this is downright sultry." He waved his hand as if fanning himself and affected his best Deep South accent. "I declare, it's not the heat. It's the humidity."

What had she gotten herself into? Easy answer to that one. She loved a challenge. Two of them stood right in front of her—the ancient inn that looked like its charm had been rubbed off, and not in a Velveteen Rabbit way, and the guy she'd tried to convince herself she could live without.

"Cold?" Elliot asked.

Definitely not. He was definitely not cold. Nope. Not at all.

"You shivered," he said. "Want a warmer jacket? When the sun ducks behind a cloud in a Wisconsin spring, we dive right back into late winter again."

Elliot rubbed his palms up and down her flat-to-her-sides arms. "Better yet," he said, "let's get inside. We can take a tour of the"—he tilted his head to one side—"estate later."

Piper nodded. *Nodded*. Smooth. A marketing specialist who'd lost all her words. *Find at least a few of them before he thinks you're—*

"Watch your step."

Too late. Her toe had already caught a lip of heaved sidewalk. She didn't sprawl, exactly. She caught herself, with a little help from Mr. Velvet Voice. "I wonder if you've thought about pavers for this front walk. Like, cobblestone-ish?"

Elliott bumped her luggage over the lip of concrete. "Long-range plans. Currently, the budget will allow for an improvement list that fits on a single square of toilet paper."

"Nice analogy," she said, navigating the wide steps to the double front door.

"I narrate audiobooks. I don't write them."

"Fair enough."

Piper steeled herself. *Resolved: Don't let his nearness distract you from the task at hand. Get this inn on the map—or navigation app.*

Two equally tough assignments, it appeared. The "how" to both of those resolutions remained a mystery.

∽ CHAPTER TWO ∾

Elliott tucked Piper's luggage away at the base of the massive staircase—one of the finer elements of the inn that remained not only intact, but a showpiece. He'd let Piper choose which of the seven remaining rooms she preferred. But first things first.

"You still a honey-in-your-tea person?" He waved to her to follow him to the kitchen.

"Yes."

"That didn't sound enthusiastic. You haven't turned vegan on me, have you?"

"Elliott. Vegan isn't a bad thing."

"I'm not wearing my 'I have the meat sweats' T-shirt today, but believe me, I own one." He didn't dare glance at that bright face to see if she fell for it. Not that he was afraid to look at her. His resolve was strong. This was a business arrangement only. Whatever he'd felt for Piper over the years had no place getting in the way of the need of the moment—Inn Rescue.

"I'm a veggie lover, but not vegan," she said. "And, as a quick reminder, tea is plant-based…as in tea leaves. Grows on bushes."

"But you're not into tea anymore?"

"I paused maybe a nanosecond and now you think I hate tea?"

"Retract your claws, Piper. It's an occupational hazard. In my line of work, a pause better have a reason or it's just dead air.

No offense intended. Let me start over. Would you like a cup of tea?"

"Hang on."

"And this pause means…?"

"What a gorgeous room! The light is stunning in here."

Okay, yes. The inn had more than one fine feature. The dining room's who-knew-how-old chandelier would improve the look of any room, but especially when the sun shining through the multi-paned windows made the crystals dance and spread a ballet of light over the surface of the mahogany table. *Ballet of light.* Had he read that in one of his projects? Not exactly his normal way of describing the luminescent dots that seemed to skate on the nearly bare table-top. "It's one of my favorite rooms."

Piper ran her slim fingers over the mahogany. Dots of light spread across her hand. She craned her neck toward the ceiling and said, "Tell me the history of the chandelier."

"History? I don't know. I think it's always been part of the inn. I probably should have asked. Maybe Gram has a hidden stash of info about things like that around here somewhere."

"Not that we need to discuss marketing strategy already, but what people see from the street level is not what they'll find inside this building. Who would know elegance like this is hiding behind those front doors?"

"An 'embarrassment'—you might say—of riches." Elliott pushed against the swinging door into the kitchen. "It'll probably be good for me to see this place through your eyes. I'm afraid I've been noticing its faults and cracks in the plaster and viewing it as my grand-mother's albatross for too long. Again, tea or…?"

She joined him in the kitchen. "I still love tea, depending on the time of day...but would it be ridiculous for me to ask if you have cold brew coffee?"

He grabbed his heart as if he'd been shot.

"Elliott?"

"Die-hard cold brew fan. New passion." Maybe passion wasn't the precise word he should have used. Voice acting and narration came easily to him. Conversation with humans? Not so much. "How do you take yours?" He opened the cupboard door to the right of the farmhouse sink and extracted two glasses.

"This time of day," she said, settling into a chair at the small round table near the window, "straight up. Lots of ice."

"I have oat, soy, coconut, or—a Wisconsin favorite—cow."

"None, please."

"If you're lactose-intolerant…"

"I'm intolerant of doctoring great coffee."

"Oh. I see. A bit of a java snob."

"And you aren't?"

Elliott left four seconds of dead air. "I have my preferences."

"Which are—"

"Tuxedo style."

Elliott in a tuxedo. She didn't have to work hard to envision that. She remembered the Dean's ball and Elliott's surprise arrival in a trim tux when all his friends had opted for a step below business casual. The only hitch to the memory was that she was across the room and someone else slid her hand through the crook in his arm that night. Elliott and what's-her-name had broken up the next week, for reasons unknown.

Piper sipped a magnificent glass of cold brew as Elliott made like a skilled barista with his own glass. Coffee, no ice. Then he carefully poured sweet cream over the top and waited. The cream looked like the finest white glaze drizzling over a double-chocolate layer cake as gravity pulled it to the bottom of the glass. She glanced at his face. The man was in awe.

She couldn't blame him.

"Maybe I'll try that version tomorrow," she said.

"I can make you one now."

Piper shook her head, both in refusal for his extra effort and in appreciation for how the sometimes self-absorbed Elliott she'd known in college had matured into this…this…tribute to manhood. *Cool it, Piper. You have work to do.*

"I'll need to know the scoop about this inn to formulate a plan for revitalizing its presence online. What's the story?"

Elliott leaned back in his chair. "The story?"

"Come on. Every town has a story. Every building has a story. I need something to work with. Marketing is all about storytelling, you know."

Elliott smiled. "You're exactly what this place needs."

"I'll take that as a compliment rather than as patting yourself on the back for thinking of me."

His smile changed. Or was it the expression in his eyes? "This isn't the only time I've thought of you." He coughed into his elbow. "I mean, I've been watching your career take off. Impressive."

"You're no slacker yourself."

"I do okay. Usually have more projects waiting when I finish one. But..."

"Spill."

"I did?" Elliott lifted his glass and checked the well-worn oak table underneath.

"Spill the tea," she said, then sighed. "It's an expression. *Give me the tea. Where's the tea. Spill the tea. Tell me the rest of the info.* You have plenty of work, but..."

"Not sure I'm settled yet on what I want to do when I grow up. I enjoy it. A little acting. A little vocal work. And it's challenging. No question about that. But it's so inescapably solitary. It's me in a small room staring at a microphone and lines of text."

They sat in silence until a cell phone cut through the atmosphere. Piper fumbled in her pocket. "Not mine. Yours?"

Elliott punched a spot on his screen and held it to his ear. "Hey, Mrs. Finster. What's on your mind?" He leaned close to Piper and whispered, "Spilled the cold brew."

"That's not how that—" she whispered back. "Oh." She grabbed a paper towel from the countertop near the sink and swiped at the rich brown pools under her glass.

"Yes, I did hear she was visiting you. You informed me when I saw you at the grocery store in Clintonville yesterday. Uh-huh. Hope you two have a great time while she's home."

"Who's 'she'?" Piper mouthed.

He held up his index finger to signal that the answer would have to wait. "Well, you know, Mrs. Finster, I have a lot on my plate right now..."

He listened for another minute and then addressed the woman whose high-pitched voice carried well even when not on speaker mode. "Just not going to work out this time," he said. He rubbed his forehead. "No, not on the weekend either."

Piper crossed the room until she stood in the doorway from the kitchen to the dining room. Could this ruse work? Sure it could. "Excuse me, Mr. Lansing? Will you be long?" She could make her voice carry far when she wanted to. "I would like to check in, if it's not too much trouble."

Confusion reigned in his dark eyes until he caught on. "Mrs. Finster. I'm afraid I have to cut our call short. I have a guest who needs my attention. Let's save that question for another time. And...goodbye now." He ended the call before the woman had a chance to say anything more, like, "And another thing—"

"You're welcome," Piper said, fake-dusting her hands.

"You saved my bacon. Thanks."

"Bacon."

"I'll put it on tomorrow's breakfast menu."

"Great idea. Now, spill the tea on Mrs. Finster. She sounds like just the woman I need to talk to."

Elliott took a big gulp of his coffee. "I couldn't do that to you."

"Let me guess. Matchmaker?"

"Endlessly."

"Keeps her eye on everyone's business?"

"Everyone's."

"Town gossip?"

"There's more than one, but I think she's the self-appointed chairperson."

"Perfect. Best place for me to start if I'm going to uncover a story we can use to draw some attention to the inn and the town."

Elliott chuckled. "Not sure she'll 'spill' the kind of stories we'd want to advertise."

"First rule of marketing, good sir. There's no such thing as bad publicity. It's all opportunity."

After rinsing and drying his cup, he reached for a linen towel draped over a thicker and heavier than necessary towel rod. The rod rested in iron U brackets at the end of the bank of cupboards. "If you enlist Mrs. Finster's help, you're likely to discover plenty of so-called opportunities."

"We could use a good scandal," Piper said between bites of wild blueberry scone at breakfast.

Elliott startled. What was she talking about?

"Not us, weirdo. The inn. The town. Something." She used the demitasse spoon to stir her tea, though she'd added nothing that needed stirring. "Something juicy. Something more than that scratching I heard in the attic. Kind of half creaky rocking chair and half a skeleton that hadn't trimmed its toenails."

"That's Harvey."

"I thought the guy staying in the Rosewood Room was named Carlton."

"He was. Is. Sleeping in this morning. He's a regular. Gram's registry book has a spot reserved for him one night every other week."

"Traveling salesman or something?"

"I don't ask."

"Why does he choose here, of all places?"

"Thanks for the vote of confidence, Piper."

Her demitasse spoon clanked onto her saucer. "Not how I meant that to come out. But it's a curiosity, isn't it? A bit of a mystery. Hmm."

"Carlton is not much of a mystery, Piper. Sorry to disappoint you. He's a pretty ordinary guy. Quiet."

"It's always the quiet ones." She lifted her eyes to the chandelier, or maybe the ceiling beyond it. "I wonder if I can talk to him before he leaves."

"No."

"'No,' as in 'He won't have time' or as in 'Don't even think about it'?"

"Gram wouldn't want us bothering the guests." Elliott lifted the lid on the teapot as if it needed monitoring.

"So…if we want to know how to get more guests to stay here, we shouldn't talk to the guests who already do? Is that what you're saying?"

Probably sounded like it. Maybe it was the stress of knowing if he failed at this, it meant relegating his grandmother to a slim-pickings future. If he could support her himself, he would. She needed a great offer on her business if she was ever going to have a chance to retire properly and afford car insurance, haircuts, and maybe an occasional dinner out with her friends. She was young enough yet. Any profit from the sale needed to last her a long time.

"And another thing," Piper said, interrupting his this-will-never-work train of thought. "If the guy upstairs is Carlton, who's Harvey?"

"Resident squirrel."

"A pet? Or a paying guest?"

"Have to get a ladder up there one of these days. He comes in and out of the attic through a vent duct of some kind. That's the rocking chair squeak sound. He explores. Deposits a few nuts and seeds he's saving for the future. He hasn't done any real damage that I know of. Not like red squirrels. They're the worst."

"Are they?"

"That's what Gram says. She's been known to feed Harvey when she sees him out in the yard. I volunteered to call an animal-control place for her, but I think to Gram, Harvey is a lifelong guest."

"What's the lifespan of a squirrel?"

Elliott laughed. How could he not? "Piper Merrill, you ask the most intriguing questions."

"I do?"

Her expression revealed she had no idea how adorable she was. Or rather, how interesting to talk to. That was it.

"I will resist feeding Harvey," she said, "and resist—temporarily—talking to guests like Carlton the frequent flyer, as long as you'll allow me to add a guest survey to the website."

"Website. Right. We should talk."

⌒ CHAPTER THREE ⌒

Piper angled her laptop screen so Elliott could see what she'd done.

"I created a social media presence for the inn. Seriously, though, I think it needs another name. 'Main Street Inn'? How many other streets does Embarrass boast? It's not hard to find. And the name doesn't exactly evoke an emotional connection for potential visitors."

Elliott refilled his thermal tumbler—lemon and honey decaffeinated tea, the concoction he claimed was the best for vocal narration hydration. "From what I recall hearing as a kid, at one point way back in the old days, it was called the Galloway. I don't know when it became the Main Street Inn. Does it matter?"

Patience, Piper, she thought. *Just like you didn't know it takes an hour of hydration before it kicks in to benefit a vocalist's throat, he simply doesn't understand these things.* "Yes, it matters."

"What's that?" He bent over her shoulder and pointed to the screen.

"Like I said, I started a social-media presence."

"I mean *that*." His finger nearly touched the screen now, and his chest leaned against the back of her shoulder.

"You were hesitant about putting a guest survey on the website, so I added it here."

"You already have survey responses?" He stepped away, and she could breathe again.

Piper enlarged the screen. "A few."

"We talked about it at breakfast, and now, half an hour later, you have it up and running?"

"Time is money, Elliott. In this case anyway."

"You're amazing."

"I'm determined."

"Sticking with my first comment. And what's all that?"

"We're getting some chatter already about my posting a photo contest. I added the image I took this morning, and yes, I doctored it just a little with some carefully placed scrollwork. I asked for anyone who has images from years past to add them and the date, and those who contribute will have their name entered into a drawing for a special prize package."

"Which is...?"

"TBD."

"To be determined? How are you getting any responses?"

"The word *free* works every time."

Elliott snagged a clementine from the fruit basket. "Want one?"

"A *free* clementine? Or does it come out of my salary?"

"Very funny."

She held out her hands, baseball-glove style, and he tossed her one.

"Hey, while you were up getting your sound room ready, Carlton left. I tried to tell him to hold on, that I'd get you so he could settle his bill and all. But he said it was 'taken care of per usual,' wished me a good day, and took off. I thought I should stop him, but if he's a regular, I assumed you either had his credit card number or he'd prepaid. Tell me I didn't just let him scam us. You. Your grandmother."

"I'm sure it's fine."

"Elliott, do we need to have a little chat about profit and loss? If you rent out a room, you should probably collect the fee for said room. Work with me here."

"Gram said if he ever leaves abruptly, check under his pillow."

Piper gasped. "That's not at all creepy."

"I think it's his way of making sure we do our duty and change the sheets between guests."

"Elliott!"

"Or…it's his way of avoiding talking to people, especially those who ask a lot of questions. Come on. Come with me."

Piper followed him to the grand staircase with two landings. "We are not seriously going to look under the guy's pillow." She didn't scurry, exactly, but she was not about to let too much distance grow between her and the shield walking ahead of her.

"You have nothing to worry about."

"Just so you know, I have my finger poised over 911 on my cell phone."

They approached the Rosewood room. Its door stood open a crack.

"Elliott, this is how it starts. This is how all the 'let's check out this suspicious-looking partly opened door' detective movies start. And then they go in with their guns drawn and no lights on and then they say, 'Clear' and the next detective goes to the back bedroom and says, 'Clear' as if a creep wouldn't hear them say that, and then *bam*! No, it was *not* clear. Elliott…"

He swung the door wide and crossed to the rosewood bed and stopped. After giving her a sidelong glance, he slowly pulled on the pillow closest to them and turned it over. "There. See?"

She stood behind him, clutched his biceps because that was typical of strong detective women, and peeked around him. There on the bed lay a clear ziplock bag full of cash.

"He pays in cash? Who does that?"

"Carlton," Elliott said flatly.

"That's it, then. It's drug money."

"Piper."

"Who leaves a wad of cash in an unlocked room?"

"Who would look for a wad of cash in an unlocked room?"

"Okay. Point taken. But—"

"I wish Gram could see you right now. You're shaking."

"Something's not adding up."

Elliott pulled one of her hands toward him and dropped the bag into her palm. "Would you mind setting this on the counter in the kitchen? I'll log it in later. Right now, I need to get to the studio. Somebody has to pay for the social media ad I'm sure you're going to want to run."

For a minute, she wondered how much it would cost to rent a drug-sniffing canine for a day. She wasn't about to stay in the room after Elliott left. Time to start a "this doesn't add up" file on her laptop.

And to rid herself of the contraband money in her hand. And find the industrial-strength hand sanitizer.

His morning's work was a study in do-overs. He rarely had this much trouble focusing. It was part of what made him good at what he did. Too much stress? Too little sleep? Too many scones? Too many thoughts of a certain exasperating genius who might come up with a way to save his grandmother's future and mess with his own?

What was he talking about? He hit the pause button again and found the spot where he'd fumbled. Took a deep breath. Shook his head to clear the thought. Why had no one told him that trick never worked?

Piper, maybe what I should have done is ask for your recommendation for someone else you know who's a marketing mastermind.

That wouldn't have been awkward at all. He shook his head again, apparently not having learned his lesson the first time.

"Mrs. Finster? Yes, this is Piper Merrill. Thanks for taking my call. I've been hired by Elliott Lansing for marketing and social media work related to the Main Street Inn."

A higher-pitched-than-necessary voice answered. "He's such a nice young man! We don't see enough of him."

Nor do I. "Yes, he is a nice young man."

"So much in common with my daughter, even though there's a slight age difference. These days, that's not a barrier, per se. I hope those two will manage some time together before she has to leave Monday morning."

Piper took a breath. *According to Elliott, that's not going to happen. But it's not my place to say.* "Your daughter's staying with you for the weekend? Is this a bad time for me to have called?"

"Not at all."

"Good. Word has it, Mrs. Finster, that you are a wealth of information about all that's important in Embarrass. One might say, an Embarrass expert."

The woman protested…a little.

"In light of your eagerness to help wherever you can," Piper said with a little extra marketing charm, "would you be willing to chat with me sometime about the history of the town, and what you might know about the inn in particular?"

"I suppose so. Will Elliott be there? I can make sure my daughter is free at that time."

"I was thinking it would be just the two of us. You and me."

"Oh. Well…"

You have to land this, Piper. "I don't want to interrupt your time with your daughter. No need for you to come to the inn. I thought we might meet away from the inn, so we don't disturb Mr. Lansing's work schedule."

"Such a nice, *hardworking* young man. He'll make a great husb—"

"When does your daughter leave to go back to her home?"

"Not that it's any of your business, but she'll be returning to Higher Grounds."

"She works at a coffee shop?"

Mrs. Finster's throat-clearing would have set Elliott's teeth on edge. "No. She's…returning…to the recovery center." Her voice brightened with, "It won't be for long this time, though. She assures me."

"My mistake." *To comment or not to comment? That is the question.* "Did you say she leaves Monday morning? Could we meet for lunch Monday then? Is there a place in town where—?"

"I'll not meet you for lunch at one of the Embarrass taverns." Her voice ended in a gruff, faux high-society half-chuckle. "We'll need to go to Clintonville."

Piper typed *Clintonville* into her laptop. Four point five miles. She keyed in *The Living Room Coffee Shop and Vintage Decor* at Mrs. Finster's suggestion. "Sounds like a charming place for lunch. I have it on my calendar."

Perfect.

Could she juggle two mysteries at a time? What was with this Carlton guy? And how was she going to uncover a story strong enough to breathe new life into an inn on life support?

What if the two were related?

To the interwebs! as Robin Hood's crew might have said if they'd been born nine hundred years later.

Yes, Elliott. I remember your warning. We can't disturb the guests. But if he doesn't know anyone is searching for intel on him, how would that be at all disconcerting?

She keyed in Carlton's full name as listed in Grandma Peggy's handwritten registry. The unusual spelling of his surname helped narrow the field. She focused the search on the Midwest, certain if he traveled and stayed only one night each time, his sales region—if that was what he wanted to call it—couldn't be on one of the coasts.

Maybe she should have started with police records.

No need. There he was. Carlton Weebrande.

Last known residence?

Embarrass, Wisconsin.

Piper stared at the screen and the decidedly *not* Main Street address. She had no choice. She had to conduct a stakeout. Or recon mission. Why would a person who lived in Embarrass get a room at an inn located in his own town? According to Elliott, he always came alone and left alone and entertained no visitors. He stayed in his room, took his complimentary breakfast in his room, paid in cash, and troubled no one.

Plus, he was just shy of a million years old, unless he was wearing a mighty fine disguise when Piper caught a glimpse of him this morning. The drug runner idea was losing its relevance too.

If his story intersected with the history of the inn somehow, he could lead to a nugget of information they could capitalize on. Piper's mind reeled with possibilities... *Maybe he and the girl he eloped with—but couldn't tell anyone about because her old-school father hadn't given his consent—used to meet in that room every other Wednesday when her father was out of town, but then the father found out and insisted on having the marriage annulled and now Carlton makes the pilgrimage to that spot to mourn the love of his life who—*

Her mind ran out of breath. Unlikely. But stranger things had happened. His routine certainly seemed odd. It was the only lead she had to follow at the moment.

She opened her navigation app and added the address. Estimated time of arrival? Three minutes. Piper jotted a note for Elliott, if he should emerge early from his studio project, that said she'd gone out for a few things.

Behind the wheel of her rental, she paused before turning the key. The stakeout wasn't a dumb idea. Or dangerous. She'd simply drive past Carlton's place, maybe park on the other side of the street for a while and see if she could spot any suspicious activity. But she would not get involved. Certainly not. And she'd keep 911 open on her screen.

What had Elliott said? That sometimes Carlton left "abruptly"? If that wasn't suspicious, nothing was!

Note to self. Really do stop at a store to pick up a few things so Elliott doesn't think I'm the suspicious one.

She double-checked the address. Whatever she'd expected, it wasn't this modest bungalow.

The side street/county road in front of the house was wide enough for her to pull to the opposite shoulder and park. And quiet enough, she hoped, not to draw attention to herself from a rare passing vehicle. She held her cell phone to her ear so nosy neighbors, curious drivers, or a curtain-peeking Carlton would assume she'd merely followed the law and pulled over to make a call.

Five minutes of that and her arm ached. But she'd seen no activity at the house. Not even a cat dodging among the pathetically untended dying daffodils and fading tulips. Maybe if she came at the house from the opposite direction…

She laid her cell phone on the passenger seat and drove to the next easy turnaround point. Viewed from the new angle, the house was just as modest, just as neglected. A light flicked on in a high window on the side of the house, the kind of window that might be over a sink. A figure appeared.

That was Carlton, all right. The man lived a few blocks from the inn. What was going on?

Tap-tap-tap.

Piper clutched her heart and swallowed the scream climbing her throat. She powered down the driver's side window a crack. "Yes?"

"You lost? Car trouble?" The bulk of a man peering in her car window looked more like an escapee from the local nursing home than a threat.

"No. No, sir. I was…making a call." She fumbled for the phone on the passenger seat and held it up as proof.

"Good," he said, standing upright. "Be careful, though." He glanced both ways. "This time of day, traffic can be a beast." The grin that broke across his face showed a couple of important teeth missing, but his eyes lit with delight at his joke.

"I'll do that. Thanks."

She watched him cross to the other side of the road, arms pumping as he hustled his way to the opposite shoulder. He was headed closer to town central, apparently. Something about his too-new-but-in-a-thrift-shop-way jogging suit and spotless athletic shoes told her he might be walking for his health to obey his cardiac rehab team.

As if she needed more evidence, he turned back and waved to her, his medical alert bracelet glistening in the spring sun.

Piper considered offering the gentleman a ride. But by the time she'd thought through the pros and cons, he was nearly to the T where the county road joined Main Street.

To stay outside Carlton's house risked drawing too much attention to herself at this point. Time to move on. A mystery was rarely solved in its first few hours, right?

The navigation app was wrong. It took only two minutes to return to the inn. Why would a guy like Carlton choose to leave his small but perfectly fine house and pay to stay at the inn every couple of weeks? Surely there were more fascinating or exotic places he could choose for a getaway.

Could be hodophobia. Maybe he feared traveling farther than a few blocks.

Piper drove the length and breadth of Embarrass looking for a coffee shop, found none, and made a mental note to research the feasibility of a coffee shop or tearoom connected to the inn as a draw for locals and those passing through.

◇ CHAPTER FOUR ◇

Where had she gone? Elliott had expected to find Piper hard at work on her laptop, designing a new logo for the inn, or spiffing up the nearly nonexistent website. His every-hour-on-the-hour stretch break—his chiropractor insisted on it—drew him downstairs, but Piper's presence graced none of the rooms.

It surprised him that he was this disappointed she wasn't around. *Come on, dude. Granted, not in this setting, but you're well used to working solo all day every day. Shake it off.*

Wouldn't hurt to check his text messages.

Nothing.

Wait. A text from his grandmother.

I'M IN HEAVEN.

Nice try, Gram. But heaven probably has a system far superior to texting.

Maybe he'd have to break his own rule and get another cup of coffee in his system today.

Three little scrolling dots told him she was keying in another line. He waited, and waited.

Spelling doesn't count, Gram. Just send it.

MADE IT SAFELY THROUGH CUSTOMS. EVELYN AND I R CRAMMING IN AS MUCH FUN AS WE CAN BETWEEN NAPS.

NICE USE OF R, GRAM. AREN'T YOU THE TECHIE.

Three more dots. TAKING PIX BUT USES LOTS OF DATA TO SEND. WILL KEEP IN TOUCH.

Elliott replied that he could wait for pictures but was happy they were enjoying themselves.

SHOULDN'T YOU BE WORKING?

He shook his head. Moms were said to have eyes in the back of their heads. Grandmothers, apparently, had global vision.

OH! FRIDAY TODAY. DON'T FORGET LAVERNE. DID I TELL U ABOUT HER? LOVE U LIKE THE OCEAN.

Laverne? Another matchmaking scheme? And how exactly does the ocean love?

A solid rap at the back door tore him away from that conundrum. Another rap sounded before he could reach the doorknob.

"Hey," the teen girl standing on the threshold said.

"Hey to you." Collecting for a school fundraiser? Neighbor kid with a complaint of some kind? Lost her puppy?

"Laverne," she said.

"Oh. I'm Elliott."

The young woman eased past him into the back hall then moved to the kitchen.

"You're...welcome to come in," he said lamely. He hadn't expected a weighty name like Laverne to belong to a ripped-jeans wearing, slouchy-sweatered girl like the waif who'd breezed by him as if she owned the place.

She snatched her hair into a high ponytail secured with a scrunchie previously circling her wrist. "You gonna be here this whole time?"

"I'm staying for a few weeks. Name's Elliott."

"You said that already. Peggy's only grandchild, right?"

"That's right."

She opened the cupboard under the sink and withdrew a caddy of supplies.

"Did you need something?" he asked. *Flummoxed*. That was what his grandmother would have called him right now.

"Kinda wouldn't mind if you disappeared."

"Excuse me? Laverne…" Nope. It didn't sound any more fitting out loud than it had in his brain.

"You do know I'm here to clean the place."

Cleaning lady. Girl. "Shouldn't you be in school?"

"Should. Tell my mom that almost every day. Although, if I wasn't homeschooled, I wouldn't have as much time to work and start saving for college."

"You're homeschooled?"

"Didn't I just say that?"

"I'm sorry. You caught me off guard."

She disappeared into the back hall and returned with a long-handled duster, a bucket, and a giant, economy-size jug of vinegar. "Your grandmother didn't mention me?"

"Mentioned." Torn between annoyance at having a teenaged human to work around and gratitude that it wasn't his responsibility to clean the place, Elliott drew a breath. "Glad you're here, Laverne." Still didn't sound right. "I'll get out of your hair."

She pulled out one earbud she'd just installed. "What?"

"Heading upstairs to work."

"Oh. Good."

"How long do you think it will take?"

"I should be out of here by four."

His eyebrows must have given away his incredulity.

"It's a big house. Besides," she said, "the slower I go, the faster my college fund increases."

So that was how she played it.

"Dude, I'm kidding." She limbered up as if prepping for a 5K. "I'm as efficient as they come. But there's lots to do. You're a sound guy or something?"

"Audio narrator. Voice actor."

"Cool. I'll save the vacuuming until you're done for the day or take a break."

"Thanks. I appreciate it."

"Oh, and I brought my own soda, knowing how evil your grandmother thinks the stuff is. You won't report me, will you?"

In some ways, Laverne reminded him of Piper. A little edge of sass wrapped around a good heart. "I won't tell. If you don't report me for absolutely, positively, needing a second cup of coffee this morning."

"Deal," she said, and popped the earbud back in.

Piper settled for a bottled latte from the cooler in the food section of the dollar store. This was certainly not the most glamorous job she'd had. But, on the other hand—Elliott.

She grabbed cans of tomatoes, black beans, cannellini beans, kidney beans, and a couple of spices from the nearby aisles on her way to the checkout. It didn't look like they'd be eating out every night. Maybe she could pull out her broke-college-student skills and whip together something for supper.

Plus…

Who better to interview than a not-very-busy checkout person in a small town? Piper guessed the woman was in her midthirties. Dressed a little upscale for a dollar store. Hmm. *Recently divorced. Kids in school during the day, but she needs a little extra income now. Or a lot…*

"Did y'all find everything ya needed?"

So much for locating someone who'd lived there all her life and knew Embarrass like the back of her hand. This woman had *Southern Living* written all over her.

"I believe I did," Piper said. "You don't sell…meat…do you?"

"Sure do. Just leave yer stuff there on the roller belt thingee and foller me."

Piper "follered" her to a section of the grocery aisles she'd bypassed.

"You got yer canned chick'n, yer baby shrimps, and then this here." The woman grabbed a can of generic beef stew. "What suits ya?"

Piper paused as long as she politely dared. "I'll take the stew."

"Good choice. My Darrel loves that stuff."

"Your husband?"

"My rottweiler."

It came out sounding like *rawtwahluh*, but Piper got the gist.

"That dog is the reason I'm here."

Piper followed her back to the checkout counter. "Here in Embarrass?"

"Glory, no. Here at the store. Gotta keep that animal fed and dewormed, if you know what I mean."

She could imagine. Piper turned the picture on the front label of the stew away from her to avoid thinking too hard about what it meant. She pulled out her credit card and asked, "Have you lived here long?"

"Long enough. Me and my boo—"

"Husband?"

"Dog. Me and Boo Darrel moved here, let's see... Well, it was winter, so that coulda been about any month but Juuu-ly. Couldna it?"

"You're a warm-weather girl." Piper smiled. If she planned to stay longer than her current assignment, she might consider stopping in the store just for the delight of a down-south conversation.

"If you'd a told me spring was gonna be such a pokey puppy around these parts, I woulda waited to make the move until the sun wasn't so shy." The woman handed Piper a plastic bag with her groceries and her bottled coffee. "Figured you'd want this left out. Anything else I can do fer ya?"

No. The insight of someone so new to the village wasn't what she needed. She thanked the woman, stepped out of the building, and headed for her car.

Who in town would know more than a person had a right to? Now *she* sounded like she'd come from a place where the sun wasn't so shy.

The sheriff, if there was one. And the postal clerk.

That could work. *Lord, is it asking too much that she's old, as in old enough to have seen actual notes and letters and postcards and personal mail rather than just junk and flyers and political ads?*

Piper's heart sank when she entered the post office. It was charming enough. Little post boxes with combination locks lined one wall. The opposite wall that looked out on the street was mostly windows. And posters of community activities and announcements covered the narrow end wall opposite the door into the adjoining community hall.

But the smiling woman behind the counter was young enough to have been in Piper's sorority, if she'd joined one. "How can I help you this glorious spring morning? Ooh! Look! It's Robin Day!"

"What?"

"Out the window. We've been seeing just a handful of robins at a time for a few weeks, but this is Robin Day. A whole flock! It's an annual rite of passage for us. Now,"—she leaned on the counter toward Piper—"can I help you somehow?"

Piper focused on the woman's name tag. Then her face—genuine, open, warm. "Kelly?"

"Yes."

"I'm Piper Merrill. New to town, which I imagine you can guess, since you must know everyone in Embarrass."

"Comes with the job," she said in a way that revealed she wasn't complaining. "Do you need a PO box?"

"No, I'm not here permanently. Helping out someone for a few weeks."

"You're Peggy's grandson Elliott's friend, right?"

Small towns. "Yes. Doing some marketing work for the inn."

"I'm sure it could use your help." Kelly's face clouded. "I hope that didn't sound unkind. Everyone in the village would benefit if we could see new life breathed into that business."

"Glad you think so. And I wonder if you could be of assistance."

"How?"

Piper's phone thrummed in her pocket. She ignored it. "What happens to old letters, like, from a hundred years ago, if they can't be delivered for some reason? I don't want to invade anyone's privacy, but if we could pull together a heartwarming or intriguing or mysterious or curious storyline or a moment in time that we can capitalize on for the inn or for Embarrass itself…"

"I see what you did there. 'Embarrass itself.' We love plays on words like that. My husband was born in Whynot, North Carolina. You can imagine how many jokes we've heard over the years."

The door opened and closed. Kelly greeted the postal patron and turned back to Piper. "Do you mind if I take care of this quick?"

"Not at all." Piper stepped to the side and focused her attention on the community activity posters. What if she created a poster that helped townspeople think about recommending the inn to visiting family at Christmas and other holidays? *No spare bedrooms for the cousins, uncles, and grown grandkids? There's always room at the Main Street Inn.* Might need a little tweaking.

In a lobby that small, Piper couldn't help but overhear the patron ask Kelly, "Can I have Elsie's mail, please? I told her she shouldn't be planting bulbs at her age. Can't walk more than a few steps today, poor thing."

"Sure." Kelly disappeared behind her side of the bank of post boxes and emerged with a small bundle that looked like mostly advertisements. "Here you go. Thanks for being a good neighbor."

"Don't know how good I am. I gave her what for. Retrieving her mail is my penance for snapping at her, I guess. Great. More seed catalogs. That woman. A thousand years old and she still thinks she can act like a woman half her age."

"Five hundred?"

Their combined laughter said a lot about both women's character.

When Elsie's neighbor had retreated, Kelly redirected her attention to Piper. "Old letters? I've spent time over the years trying hard to locate recipients for letters misaddressed or with missing return addresses if undeliverable. A bit of detective in my DNA. But eventually, they wind up in Atlanta at the MRC—Mail Recovery Center."

"Oh." Kelly's sleuthing skills could be beneficial though.

"And it might stay sixty or ninety or a hundred and eighty days before it's recycled, destroyed, or, if it's something of value, even auctioned off if there's no way to trace the sender or recipient."

Piper's hopes of a hundred-year-old letter or two that might lead to other clues passed through her mental paper shredder.

"But you might be interested in something else I have."

Pause the paper shredder.

"The other half of this building is devoted to village council notes, archives, etc. Every once in a while, a piece of business or a mail item or a newspaper article pops up. I've kind of squirreled them away in a file. And when the village leadership decided to clean out a storage closet, I volunteered to take anything of historical significance off their hands."

"You did?"

"Just couldn't imagine getting rid of bits of trivia, even."

Piper kept herself from blurting, "I love you!" Instead, she opted for, "Interesting."

"Let me get the file so you can take a look."

When she disappeared, Piper pulled out her phone, thrumming once more. Elliott apparently hadn't found her note. The text message read:

WHERE ARE YOU? COME HOME. WE'VE BEEN INVADED!

~ CHAPTER FIVE ~

Elliott leaned back in his office chair, his arms crossed. It was considerate of Laverne to wait to vacuum until the end of his workday. But apparently cleaning a many-roomed inn meant flushing many toilets.

Noisy, noisy toilets.

What made him think he could do this—juggle the inner workings of the inn, rescue it from demise, and keep up with his career deadlines at the same time? Work from home? Not as simple as it sounded.

You have help.

Was that hopeful interior dialogue, or the inner Voice his gram talked to as if He were in the room?

Yes. I have help. Piper. He breathed deep as two women's voices rose from a floor below. Piper and Laverne.

He shot out of his chair and headed toward them, descending the masterpiece of a staircase as if he were still in middle school. He slid to a stop on the hardwood floor in the hall that led from the front door straight through to the kitchen at the back of the inn.

If Piper mentioned the "invasion" to Laverne, he might lose one of his key helpers before she finished cleaning.

"Hey, you two," he said, more than a little breathless. "Glad you're back, Piper. Did you have a chance to meet Laverne yet?"

Piper eyed him as if recommending he cut down on the caffeine. "Barely. Really happy you're here, Laverne."

"Yes, me too," Elliott said. "Grateful for the help."

Piper set a plastic bag of something on the floor. It clunked like cans. But she held tight to a manila envelope she clutched to her chest. "Oh, she will be even more help than you know. This young woman is a wealth of knowledge."

Laverne waved a dustcloth like a flag. "You can't clean people's houses without learning a few things…unintentionally." She glanced at Piper as if they'd already swapped secrets.

They couldn't have. Right? "We don't want to hold you up, Laverne. Piper, can I have a minute?"

"Sure." She grabbed the bag at her feet and headed to the kitchen. Elliott followed.

"Mr. Lansing? Okay if I vacuum upstairs now…since you're on break?"

I'm on break because you've been flushing toi—"No problem."

"I'll be quick. One good thing about not having many guests. Less mess."

Yeah. Good thing.

"Please tell me I can brew some proper tea, as the Brits say." Piper turned her head to the window, her face as pensive as he'd ever seen it. "That just might be a saving grace."

He directed his gaze out the window too. Not much was happening out there, except the maple leaves racing toward adulthood at last. And the ancient shed in the back corner of the property needed more paint than the main building. Something else for the to-do list. "What's a saving grace?"

"Tea."

"Tea's nice, but it's hardly—"

"Not a *cup* of tea, Elliott. A tearoom! Operating all year round in one of the parlors."

A youthful voice said, "This place used to serve three meals a day when it was first built, the way I hear it."

Both Elliott and Piper turned at the voice. "Laverne! I...we... thought you were upstairs," she said.

Thanks, Piper. My sentiments exactly.

"Forgot the carpet freshener I usually add to the vacuum. And I think it's a great idea." She grabbed a cardboard canister from the supply cupboard at the base of the back stairwell and flipped it end over end in one hand as if she'd practiced. "Great idea."

"The inn used to be a restaurant? I thought it was a hotel." Piper fingered the manila envelope still in her grasp.

"Both/and. See you two later." Laverne was up the stairs and out of sight before Elliott could form the question he wanted to ask.

Piper dug in the plastic bag's contents with one hand.

"What's that?"

"Supper."

"In an envelope?"

"Oh, this." She patted it as if it were a baby needing to burp. "This is gold." She abandoned the supper makings and opened the envelope. "Everything from how the town got its unfortunate name to historical records to love letters to newsletter reports from open village council meetings."

"Where'd you get all this?"

"Kelly."

"Kelly…?"

"Post office."

"Oh, *that* Kelly."

"By the way, I don't think Carlton is who he says he is. I mean, he's actually Carlton, but something's not adding up. And you know what that always means."

"We're too nosy?"

Piper huffed. "It means we're on to something. We are just a couple of stories away from having a real gem we can use to save this place and your grandma's retirement!"

Elliott chuckled.

"What?"

"You live an exclamation-point life, don't you, Piper?"

"Is that a bad thing? Are you saying I'm childish? Too much? Annoying?"

He leaned his backside against the counter. "Quite the opposite. You're a delight." *Ahk! Now who was too much?* Counters, he discovered, were horrible counselors. The one against which he leaned failed to stop him from making a fool of himself. He could blame it on Piper and her irresistibility.

No. He had to own this one. "Delight…fully enthusiastic."

She nodded slowly, the light in her eyes dimming a kilowatt or two. "I have reading to do." She indicated the envelope. "You probably have work?"

"Yes. Yes, I do. I'll…see you in a few hours, and we can talk about the tearoom idea?"

"Sure. Sounds good. Hey, Elliott. I expected to find the place overrun with mice. Or other varmints. 'We've been invaded'?"

He filed his nails on the stubble of his jawline. "Yeah, that. Laverne."

The kilowatts were back. "Elliott Lansing, you live a question-mark life, don't you?"

He opened his mouth then closed it again.

The way she tilted her head made her dark curls pool on her shoulder.

Stay that way, would you?

On second thought, I'd like to erase that question mark.

Piper scooted her tea mug a little farther away from the stack of investigative material on the scarred kitchen table. Bless Kelly's heart for photocopying the pertinent documents for her so she wouldn't have to be burdened with returning them or worried about defacing them. She could highlight all she wanted.

Interesting. A newspaper account of a now defunct local furniture manufacturer who made a living chair out of carefully planted and tended box elder trees. Could Elliott and his grandmother change the name to the Box Elder Inn? *Come sit where others sat. Feel the chair grow around you. Experience the wonders of sap. And box elder bugs galore!*

Not quite the marketing angle she was looking for.

The settlement was incorporated in 1895. Her eyes scanned more words recorded in a handwritten report. Heavy influence of French-Canadian lumberjacks in the early days of Embarrass. *The woodsmen attempted to send logs down the river and found it almost impossible because of all the many bends, twists, and snags. They called it the Riviére d'Embarras. In French, the word Embarrasser means to impede, to obstruct, or to entangle.*

"I don't need a log jam. I need something romantic! Or…" Two hearts entangled, entwined. That could work…

Page after page of the letters and news articles listed village incorporation business, prominent businesspeople, even the divided vote to incorporate. She skimmed info for a while. Then her eyes landed on a handwritten letter from someone named Martha to her grandma.

Edward E. Breed sold his land and went to Arizona to invest in gold mining.

She sipped her tea, eyes still on the page.

The venture failed.

Don't they always?

His wife Leona did not go to Arizona. She went to a nearby area and opened a store. When the railroad came through, they named the station Leona and the Post Office department also accepted that name.

Leona, Wisconsin. She'd driven through there, hadn't she? Piper checked her map app. Laona, spelled differently. It was a bit farther north of her route from the airport. Then she checked Google. Just as she feared, Martha's story wasn't quite the official one. Laona Johnson was the first child born to settlers in the area, so the town was named after her. Martha had a good imagination though.

That was one thing she couldn't imagine Elliott ever doing—leaving his responsibilities at home to follow something shiny and gold and risky. He had just enough risk within him. He'd devoted himself to giving this venture his best efforts for his grandma's sake.

In all his talk about making sure his grandmother had enough to retire without concerns, he'd never once mentioned that as her only grandchild, he might inherit the leftovers someday.

As if he hadn't given it a thought.

Who wouldn't love—

Like.

Who wouldn't like a guy who would do something like that— including using his own money to pay for her marketing expertise— without caring if he ever got anything out of it?

She considered the letter she'd just read. "Edward E. Breed, whether you're real or not, if you were lured by the glint of gold to the detriment of everyone you said you cared about, you could learn a few things from Elliott Lansing."

"That was rough." Piper ended her call and stuffed her notes along with the clippings and letters back into the manila folder.

"What was rough?" Elliott thought she'd heard him approach. Old floors squeak. But she must have been so engaged in her phone conversation that she missed the warnings. Her startle reflexes were in great shape. He rested a hand on her shoulder, as if that would help.

"I spent a very unproductive late afternoon on the phone. How did you do with your deadline?"

"A little light editing left, but it was more fruitful than what you experienced, apparently."

"Laverne left about an hour ago."

Elliott drew his hand back. "I didn't pay her."

"I tried to. She said your grandmother paid ahead for the length of her sabbatical. Laverne called it a sabbatical. What teen knows what that means? Anyway, she's been paid."

"Good. A relief in more ways than one."

Piper turned in her chair to face him fully. "Elliott, did you think you were going to be tasked with keeping this place clean too while you're here?"

"It crossed my mind."

"What's the 'in more ways than one'?"

He should stop staring at her eyes. Not helpful. "Doesn't matter. Tell me about your disappointing phone call."

"Calls. Plural. Do I sound like a threat on the phone?"

More like music. "Why?"

"I called six of the eight people Kelly recommended I talk to. People she thought might know more than the average villager about the history of Embarrass or especially about the inn's background."

"No help?"

"No talk. They all had one excuse or another why they couldn't have a conversation with me."

"I'll talk to you. You said you have ideas brewing?" He took another chair at the table she and her research material occupied.

"I do, but I should start dinner."

"You don't have to do that. We could eat out."

"Where, exactly? Not here in town."

"We'd have to drive a few miles."

"I feel like staying in tonight."

"Me too."

"Besides," she said, "I have a plan for dinner. Where would I find a colander?" She stood and rustled through upper cupboards.

"Spaghetti?"

"No. A surprise. Let's just call it Mystery Chili. I need the colander to rinse the meat."

"What?"

"Better if you don't ask. See that notebook by my phone? You'll find sketches of ideas there. We can talk while I cook. Or…assemble."

"I'm a decent cook," Elliott ventured. "I mean, if you need any help." Not that she did. When it came to capable women, Piper was—

"Never mind. Found it." She waved the colander like she'd achieved a culinary victory. "Can opener? Wait. Let me guess." She pulled open a drawer. Shut it and opened another. "Bingo!"

Solitary. He was a solitary person living a perfectly content solitary life that suited him just fine. Why then did everything seem brighter when she was in the room or the conversation?

"Notebook. Yes." He slid it closer and hummed.

"What are you humming?"

Without raising his eyes from her list, he said, "Better than clearing my throat. It isn't as hard on the vocal cords."

"Who knew?" She used the hand-crank opener to pop the tops on what looked like survival food.

"I see the tearoom idea here. Might have real possibilities." And require a ton of work.

"Imagine the dining room with clusters of smaller tables. Or maybe we'd use one of the parlors for that. Laverne said at one time, the wall between the current dining room and the second parlor didn't exist."

"All one big room?"

"That's what she said. I suppose that was to accommodate the hotel's dining guests back in the early 1900s."

Something was starting to smell good already. "How'd Laverne know that?"

"She dusts."

"I hoped she would."

Piper peered over her shoulder at him. "Including picture frames. There's a stack of unhung photos propped in a corner somewhere. Storeroom, maybe? Attic? We should investigate."

"Making a note. Ah. Text from Gram."

"Tell her I said hi."

"What time is it for her?" Elliott glanced at his watch.

Piper dug a soup pot from a lower cupboard with an *ugh*. "Tomorrow."

"She says, 'Sunshine. Glorious sunshine. We're drinking it in, Elliott. And the architecture! Seeing more museums today than in the rest of my life put together. LOL.'"

"She said 'LOL'?"

"And then a little more about the art and architecture."

"Sounds like she's having the time of her life."

Elliott ran his finger around the rim of his phone case. "She deserves every minute of it."

Piper reached for an ancient-looking apron on a hook near the back door. "She won't mind if I—"

"I'm sure she'd be honored you're wearing it. I'll tell her how adorable you—how adorable it looks on you." Elliott laughed then keyed in the words. His grandma's answer surprised him. "Huh," he said.

"What?"

"She said, 'Under no circumstances.' Then added, 'Please, no.' What could that mean?"

Piper's eyes were as round as biscuit cutters. She slipped the apron off her neck and gingerly rehung it in its spot.

"She must have misunderstood, Piper. I'll ask again."

"No. That's okay. I can use a towel. Curious, though. But every woman has a right to leave some memories out of reach. Maybe that's it for her. Cooking for your grandfather. Or maybe she was wearing it when he died."

"He's alive."

"He is? You never talk about him."

"He walked out of her life, his daughter's life, *my* life a long time ago. The day I was born, in fact. I had no father in my life because he chose not to be. No grandfather either. And then I had a grieving grandmother. Mom had a hard time rising above my father's betrayal and my grandfather's self-absorbed reasons for leaving. Grandma said I was her reason for going on."

"Then when your mom died…"

"Yeah. I thought I was old enough to take care of myself by then." He sighed. Sorrow would fester if it wasn't exhaled. "Turns out my grandma and I became each other's reasons."

Wooden spoon pressed to her heart, Piper said, "I can't wait to meet her someday." Then she acted like she'd committed a gross faux pas. A stunned look on her face, she added, "If…if I'm still here when she gets back from her trip. That's what I was thinking."

Piper turned to the stove and dipped the spoon into their mystery supper.

∾ CHAPTER SIX ∾

Piper watched Elliott scrape the bottom of his bowl for the last morsel of Make-Do Chili.

"Excellent," he said.

She side-eyed him.

"Too much? It was certainly…filling."

"Still trying too hard," she said, but had to give him credit for finishing a second helping. Her gaze darted to the apron hanging in the corner.

"You're not offended by Gram's feelings about that apron, are you?"

"No. Not offended. But I wonder what it is about it that evoked such a strong response from her. It's the story, you know. The story is the thing we're missing. What if…?"

"A wild imagination is a beautiful thing to watch."

"Humor me, Elliott. Why would she leave it hanging there if she didn't want anyone to touch it?"

"It has to be an antique."

"Probably is, judging by how faded the fabric is."

"A collectible?"

"Elliott. It hangs by the back door of a kitchen no guest sees. Does that sound like a collectible to you?"

"All grandmothers are entitled to their eccentricities."

"I guess so." She wasn't going to be deterred by a nonexplanation though. Somehow, she'd figure it out. But top priority right now was saving the inn in which the apron hung.

"Should we do some kind of event that would tie in to the barn quilts?" she asked. "With so many barn quilts in Sha-*wan*-o County…"

"First question, what's a barn quilt? And it's *Shaw*-no."

"There's another *a* in the word. Thus, another syllable."

"Not if you live around here."

"*Shaw*-no. Got it. You've seen barn quilts if you've visited this area. My knowledge of them comes completely from online sources, but you must have seen those—"

"Are you talking about the giant quilt squares painted on the end of barns where the haymow door is? I've seen a few."

"Elliott, there are hundreds in *Shaw*no County." She emphasized her corrected pronunciation. "Imagine tapping into the quilting craze."

"Quilting is a craze?"

"My point is that a tour of the local barn quilts could be a big draw."

She pushed her bowl away and drew her notes closer. "There's no time to pull a tour together for this spring, but maybe summer. If something's on the books, scheduled, it gives us fodder for social media posts, images for the website…"

"We could do a day trip, the two of us, to take pictures of the barns for publicity materials," Elliott said. "Who first started painting quilt squares on them?"

"I know the answer to that. In 2010, a guy named Jim Something-or-other got the idea to have groups sponsor or create these brilliantly colored barn quilt squares to help draw attention to the area, spotlight the county's historic barns and the need for preservation, and to give groups an opportunity for a service project. Like 4H clubs, community organizations, quilting guilds."

"He invented the idea?"

"No. He'd seen quilt squares on barn gable ends in other states and in southern Wisconsin. But Elliott, there are over 400 barn quilts around here now. Just a few miles away. That's a gold mine we might be sitting on if we could— Oh! Quilter retreats with a coach tour of the barn quilts. We could decorate all the little tables in the dining room—"

"Little tables which we don't have yet."

"—with quilt table coverings and quilt supplies and whatever. Connect with quilters' groups. Offer a discount if a quilt group books the entire inn."

"Could work."

"And that wouldn't take as much lead time to organize. Or…"

Elliott placed his palms on the tabletop. "Should I brace myself for this one?"

"Quilters and history go together. They love the history behind the patterns, the fabrics, the concept of how even with very little with which to work, women have always wanted to make things beautiful and keep their families warm. Oh, the stories quilts tell."

"Where are you going with this?"

"You."

"Me?"

"The storyteller."

"At a quilt retreat."

"Exactly! Picture it. The quilters have spent the day enjoying barn quilts and working on new projects. After a lovely meal at the Whatever Its Name Is Inn, they all gather in the parlor around a glowing fire, if it's cool enough, or a bunch of candles in the fireplace, and hear tale after tale of the inn's background and the romantic and ever-so-charming logging history of the area from no other voice than the famous Elliott Samuel Lansing."

"Who's he? My middle name's Billingsly."

"What? It is not."

"You're right. It's Samuel. I didn't know you knew that."

"I may or may not have checked to make sure you didn't have a criminal record before agreeing to work for you."

"Smart. One never knows." He leaned in conspiratorially and narrowed his eyes. "What did you find out about the guy?"

Not fair. His eyes that close. His voice near enough to fan the peach fuzz on her cheeks. "His…his breath smells like meat. Not that it's a bad thing." She glanced at his lips then pushed away from the table.

"About his criminal record," Elliott whined, although a voice that rich had a hard time pulling off a whine.

"Clean. Clean record. Not even a traffic violation. And now, I shall clean up this mess." She threw the flour sack towel from the rack at the end of the counter over her shoulder and turned to the sink.

The towel slid off her shoulder, not of its own volition. "Let me do the cleanup," Elliott said. He pointed to her head. "Your imagination station must be tired."

She spread her arms wide and lifted her face to the heavens, far above the pressed tin ceiling. Her heart chanted *He does dishes. He volunteers to do dishes!*

"Happy?" he asked.

Very.

Elliott turned away from the sink as if it had stung him. "I... we...I have guests checking in late tonight. I do. Well, Gram does. We?" He should have expected Piper's laughter over his "question mark life."

"Let's say *we*," Piper countered. "We're in this reclamation project together. How can I help?"

"I've been so consumed with concern about drumming up more business that I completely forgot about tending to the few guests that already do show up, rare as they are. While you were gone today, I looked over the reservation book Gram uses. By checking in late, I mean late. The couple is booked for two nights, but they're not arriving until close to midnight, according to Gram's note."

Piper stood from the paper-strewn table and stretched. "We have time, then. What needs to be done?"

"Laverne did most of it, bless her. The room's ready. Fresh sheets and towels."

"I can pick some daffodils for their room, if I can find any that aren't too far gone. That would be a nice touch."

Elliott glanced at his smartwatch then out the window. "Piper, it's almost dark out there."

"Do you think it would be the first time I've picked flowers in the dark?"

"Yes."

"You'd be right. But I have this." She raised her phone and clicked on the blinding flashlight feature. "Perfect accessory for midnight garden raids."

"The guests are honeymooning over in Norway. Couldn't get the cottage they wanted until Sunday. Instead, they found this place."

"Several questions. How? *How* did they find this place? And two, how are they getting from here to Norway? And three…"

"The *town* of Norway in Michigan's Upper Peninsula."

"Oh."

"Named for the Norway Pines in the area back in the late 1800s when the town was formed."

"And they're honeymooning there because…?"

Elliott wiped the stovetop with a damp paper towel. "Some things must remain a mystery forever."

"Or we could ask them."

"Piper. *Honeymooners.* I think they probably would like to be left alone while they're staying. We're… I'm… Gram is an innkeeper, not an investigative reporter. That makes us—"

"Curious innkeepers."

He chuckled. "You can say that again. I'm out of my element here. In some ways."

"And right where you need to be in others," she said. "I'll try to reserve my intense grilling of the guests until and unless they reveal they want to talk."

"Piper—"

"Which gives me a great idea. Is the inn on any of the guest review sites online?"

"I don't know."

"We need to make sure. I may be able to tap into some of those reviews to get us snippets we can use in social media marketing. Talking to happy past guests. It's an avenue I hadn't considered until now." She tapped a few keys on her laptop. Then a few more. "We have to get the inn a presence on these sites."

Elliott headed toward the butler's pantry. If Gram had one of her famous quiches in the freezer, it would solve the problem of what to serve for breakfast, providing the newlyweds wanted breakfast in the morning. "I agree," he said, loudly enough to be heard back in the kitchen proper.

"But we need a better name. And logo. Tell me this. If you were searching online for someplace special…"

Two quiches. Roasted red pepper and kale, or potato, baby Swiss cheese, and broccoli. The potato.

"…and your choices were cozy and charming with a charming name…"

His eyes caught a rare skiff of dust Laverne had missed. He set the frozen quiche on the marble surface of the pantry's built-in cupboard. *What's that?*

"…or a high-priced minimalist number with a one-word name, like Sterling…"

Picture frames. Aha!

"…or a little-known inn on Main Street in Embarrass, Wisconsin, with a name like the Main Street Inn, which would you choose?"

"This one," Elliott said. He set a stack of ancient picture frames and their images on the kitchen island. "Take a look. I need to retrieve tomorrow's breakfast before I forget about it."

"You're going to the store?"

"I'm going to Gram's preplanning center." He indicated the opening to the butler's pantry.

Moments later, he was back with the quiche and more hope than he'd had in a while.

Piper was bent over the photos, studying them. "Are these the pictures Laverne was talking about?"

"I think so."

"I love this watercolor painting of the inn. The soft shading. The detail. It's so unique, as if blending what must have been its early beginnings on the right half of the painting with more modern day on the left. Both time periods merging seamlessly. Elliott, is that your grandma and grandpa on the left?"

He came closer. "That's definitely Gram. I've only seen a handful of pictures of him, but that looks like my grandfather beside her."

"He looks a little like you, but his face is…harder. Like cement. How did the artist capture that in watercolor?"

"That would have been before Grandpa left her."

"Your grandma seems wistful."

"She does."

"Almost as if she's looking back at history and longing for something she doesn't have. I wonder if this sweet couple on the right could be the original owners."

"You're not the only one who wishes we had access to more of the history of this place."

"Elliott."

"What?"

"Let me grab my phone. Okay, stand right there." She slid close to him. "Put your arm around my shoulder."

"What?"

"Please."

She didn't have to ask twice. "A selfie?"

"Humor me. Now, lean your head down toward me, and I'll look up at you."

"Like this?"

Piper tried to see her phone screen without moving her head. "We'll give it a try. Okay, somber but tender look."

You're killing me, here, Piper. "Somber but tender, huh?"

Her gaze, that delicate face upturned. Without moving his lips, he spoke through closed teeth. "How long am I supposed to hold this pose?"

Her lips parted but no sound came out.

He heard the camera click. Then again.

She blinked hard and turned her attention to the image she'd tried to capture. She laid it next to the watercolor on the island. "That's crazy, isn't it?"

"Crazy," he said. "If we wore period costumes, and if I put on more than a few pounds, and if your hair was a different color, and if I owned a beaver skin hat, and if you had plastic surgery to make your nose look more like that woman's, we'd be the spittin' image of the two of them."

"Elliott!"

"Piper, I love your imagination, but except for their height differences, and…and his arm around her, they don't look anything like us."

"They do too, and you're just being difficult."

"Am not. I'm being realistic and logical."

"And that's how fights start that break up relationships," she said under her breath.

"We don't have a relationship." *You use your mouth and voice for a living, Elliott. One would think you would know how to converse by now. That wasn't it.*

Piper stepped back. "You're right, of course."

"But friendship is a…a relationship."

She raised her chin just a touch. "It is. Grateful for it. Why don't you make whatever preparations you need for our…your guests, and I'll study these other pictures to see if I can find clues that will give us a story we…*you* can use."

Does idiot have two Ts?

∽ Chapter Seven ∾

The "newlyweds" were in their fifties and chattier than Elliott would have predicted. Piper was in her element listening to them talk, but a more subdued version of Piper. He was to blame. No getting around it.

She'd insisted on waiting up with him until the guests arrived. As awkward as that was with the two of them a little too obviously trying to stay out of each other's way, he had to admit he was grateful she'd volunteered. Piper was a master at making conversation with strangers. In his line of work, he could count on the delete feature of his editing software.

Within minutes of their arrival, Piper and Elliott knew most of the couple's love story. It was a second honeymoon trip for them for their silver anniversary. They owned a family cottage near Norway, Michigan—the town where the husband was born—but now rented it out part of the year to help cover upkeep and taxes. They teased each other over whose fault it was that the cottage was booked the weekend they'd wanted it for themselves. But the teasing held humor rather than animosity.

"That's how you make something last," Piper said. "Find a way to laugh about it, right?"

Elliott waited for her to look his way, but she didn't.

Guess he deserved that.

"I'm curious," she said at a break in their litany of tales. "How did you happen to choose the Main Street Inn in Embarrass?"

The husband nudged his wife.

"When we were trying to decide how we could cut the trip to Norway in half, since we'd be getting such a late start, we drew a line between our home and the cottage. The line crossed right through Embarrass, and that seemed more than fitting, under the circumstances."

"Sounded like a God-thing to me," the husband said. "And that pretty well describes our whole marriage to now."

Elliott ventured into the conversation. "You booked the Maple Room."

"It was the cheapest one available," the two said in unison.

Elliott turned to Piper. "Would you mind opening up the Lumber Baron's suite?"

"I think that's a great idea," she said, tapping her palm against her heart.

"A suite? No. We couldn't—"

"Same price," Elliott said. "It just seems as if a marriage like yours deserves a little luxury tonight. I know my grandmother. She'd insist."

By the time Elliott showed them to their suite, Piper had not only opened the room, she'd moved the vase of lily-of-the-valley—daffodils had passed their prime—from the Maple Room, dimmed the lights, and started a small fire in the suite's fireplace. The luggage rack was open and waiting. Foil-wrapped chocolates lay on the pillowcases, and the bed was turned down.

"Oh, this is lovely," the wife said. "More than we ever expected."

"Breakfast is on your timetable tomorrow, given the lateness of the hour," Elliott said. "I'll need about forty-five minutes of a heads-up, if you don't mind."

"We don't want to put you out any more than we already have with the late check-in and everything," the husband protested.

"It would be a pleasure," Piper said before Elliott could.

He nodded once. "Indeed."

The husband took his wife's hand in his.

"We'll leave you to enjoy the rest of your evening then," Elliott said, backing toward the door.

At the bottom of the stairs, he turned. "That it is. I can close up. Douse the lights. Lock up. Should we say good night?"

Piper was on the next-to-the-last step, which put them almost at eye level. She cupped his head in her hands, drew it to her, and planted a kiss on his forehead. "Thank you for being generous when you can't afford to be, my…friend. Good night."

Elliott went through closing duties. She'd only been gone a few minutes, but somehow he felt the absence. He checked the back entrance one more time. Locked tight. What else did he need to do? Program the coffee maker for the morning, which was approaching much too quickly.

He stopped at the kitchen table. Those images. If he was careful, could he remove the backing of the framed watercolor to see if it told more? If his grandmother and grandfather were in the painting, they had to have been the ones to commission it. The signature on the bottom right of the painting was illegible. Maybe the back held more information.

Only a penciled date. A month before his birth. Thirty days later, his grandfather wouldn't have been in the picture any longer. Had his grandmother known? Suspected? Who would have painted it? And how could Gram have afforded to commission a piece of art like this?

God's doings sometimes disguise themselves as coincidences, Elliott.

He could hear his grandmother's voice in his head.

This already didn't feel like a coincidence.

Piper slept more soundly than she thought possible, given all the ideas racing through her mind. A typical marketing campaign might take weeks to formulate and months or years to implement. They didn't have that kind of time.

When she lost the battle with the beam of sunlight that fought its way around the outer edges of her room's shade, she got up, showered quickly, and dressed in her best detective outfit, which looked a lot like what she wore to the gym, including the shoes. It was going to be a pound-the-pavement kind of day.

The aroma of coffee pulled her down the back stairs to the kitchen, at one time likely the servants' stairs. The room was empty, but lights on the coffee maker proudly boasted it had done the job without human intervention.

The photographs and watercolor still lay on the kitchen island. The images had to hold at least a few clues. They seemed out of chronological order, with improvements and upgrades to the property on some, then older pictures from before the changes. Some were dated, others weren't. She chose randomly and studied an image of the interior of the inn in a more opulent time period. Must have been the 1890s.

What looked like heavy velvet drapes hung at the windows. Dark paneling made the room feel almost cave-like, but it was lit from above with two grand chandeliers. A collection of Victorian furniture crowded the room as if excess would make a room more inviting.

Ah. An older image. Horses tied at the rail. She sipped her coffee. The facade of the building was plainer in this image. Flatter, if that was the right word. Except for…

Interesting. She pulled her phone from her pocket and tapped the magnifier feature. What was that? A stump? One of those stool things to climb up on a horse? No, too tall. And it had a definite shape. It looked like a moose head. With…she leaned in closer…a butterfly on its nose?

Couldn't be. She snapped a picture of the image to enlarge later. What she thought she saw had to be an optical illusion.

She laid the frames out in a grid pattern, chronologically as best as she could figure.

"Find anything interesting?"

That voice. It could calm a troubled sea and stir a tempest of emotions at the same time. He stood beside her now, observing the grid she'd created.

"Notice anything unusual, Elliott?"

He peered closer. "Some are duplicates of pictures already hanging in the main rooms, aren't they?"

"Or almost the same. Notice anything about the background on these?"

He was silent for a few moments. "The trees. There are trees in the background in the earlier images. Not as many in these later ones." He stood. "Practically none now, except for the row across the rear of the property."

"Might have lost a lot of them to Dutch Elm disease?"

"Could be. What made you think of that?"

"My dad's a landscape designer."

"We've been talking a lot about my family. Not much about yours."

"It's hard to talk about them."

"I'm sorry."

"No, Elliott. Don't be sorry. It's hard to talk about them with people like you because my family is all kinds of wonderful. I think I have a touch of survivor's guilt, because I don't hate my parents, they didn't ruin my life, and I know I can always count on them. See? That look on your face. So many people are struggling with their heritage, and I'm overly blessed. It's—"

"An embarrassment of riches, as they say? This look," he said, "is not jealousy or fresh pain or a sign that you 'triggered' something from my past. Maybe it's because I haven't shaved yet this morning. It was supposed to reflect an expression of gratitude. You reminded me that my mom loved me, despite her struggles, and that I always, always have had the consistent love and support of Grandma Peggy. I'm overly blessed too. And then there are...friends like you."

She let her gaze drift to his jawline. "Don't shave."

"What?"

"Never mind. Okay, the pictures. As the years advanced, the trees disappeared, maybe because the logging industry wanted to make sure they got them all."

"It was a different time, that's for sure. Today, they'd replant faster than they harvest."

"There's something else though. Look closely." She stepped back so he could get a better view.

His eyes scanned the grid then returned to several images. "What's that?"

"It's here in this first photo then again in this next one. And this one. Then it's gone. Except…"

"Except what?"

"Look at the watercolor again. It's faint, but what do you see behind the historical couple?"

"Same shape?"

"I'd say so. See the sign hanging on the front of the building on this other image? Looks like it was taken in the '40s or '50s. Sweet vintage cars in the foreground. It's hard to read, but the sign has this same shape on it."

"The tree stump with arms?"

"They're antlers."

"Antlers?"

"Moose antlers. Here." She clicked on the magnifier app again.

"Is that a—"

"Butterfly. Yes."

Elliott squinted. "What's a butterfly doing on a moose's nose? I suppose it happens, but talk about your weird friendships."

"It's symbolic of something. Strength and gentleness?"

"Doesn't really fit the image of a hotel though. In a lumbering community."

"True. Unless…"

Elliott's phone dinged. Text message.

"The honeymooners are awake," he said. "They'll be down in forty-five minutes. How willing are you to assist with breakfast?"

"Completely."

"That's what I hoped you'd say. Would you kindly set up the small table by the front window in the parlor? Tablecloth, napkins, silverware…"

"Lily-of-the-valley?"

"Great idea. I'll get the quiche warming and cut up fruit for the parfaits."

"You make parfaits?"

"Who doesn't?"

Piper rolled her head like a combo of yes and no. "Where do I find the—"

"Everything you need is in the butler's pantry. Gram marked it all."

"I'm on the case."

Elliott stopped moving long enough to smile at her. "You always are."

The last pieces of leftover quiche started the day off right on Monday. It had been a great weekend, as far as Piper was concerned. More relaxing than she'd imagined it would be. It took a little arm-twisting, but she finally admitted Elliott was right. They both needed a break from the constancy of their responsibilities.

After the honeymooners checked out Sunday morning, they'd done minimal cleanup then headed to the church Elliott attended with his grandmother when he was in town. They'd had to drive to New London, south of Clintonville, which meant it wouldn't have done much good to corner parishioners after the service and pepper them for information.

She focused on what she needed more than info. The music, the sermon, the sweet fellowship. And it didn't hurt that Elliott hovered close.

They'd lunched in Clintonville at Adelle's Bluebird Café—chicken soup and homemade dumplings with a lemon cream pie chaser. Elliott insisted they return for the Friday night fish fry sometime before she left.

The one second it took him to say "before you leave" was the low moment of the weekend. In a few weeks, she'd be back at her normal nine-to-five, in her ordinary apartment in a city with an ordinary name. She liked her life. Elliott's comment shouldn't have hit her as hard as it did. She dismissed it more quickly than she downed the pie, which was saying something.

They'd decided to make the most of the warmer temps and fresh air and the opportunity to walk off a few calories. Piper resisted taking notes but mentally recorded her observations as the two walked the length and breadth of Embarrass. Where was her missing link?

She was confident something would pop up in street names or other century-old buildings. But few buildings that old—homes or businesses—remained. They lingered on the bridge over the Embarrass River, no more than a city block from the inn. The water level was higher than it would be midsummer, Elliott had told her, but it still seemed quiet and serene and almost unremarkable to Piper.

The twists and turns that had bothered the lumberjacks trying to float logs down the river were as obvious as they must have been 120 years earlier. Banks were tangled with wildflowers and brambles. Unsophisticated but beautiful in their own way.

"From the sky," Elliott said, "the river looks like the varicose veins on an old man's legs."

"Old man's?"

"That's what Gram told me after her hot-air balloon ride."

"I've always thought that would be fun—going up in a hot-air balloon."

Elliott stared into the river. "Did you know that if you traced this water far downstream, it eventually empties into other rivers that empty into Lake Michigan, which means that because of the Great Lakes connection, that drop of water right there might wind up pouring over Niagara Falls?"

Piper admitted it was hard to imagine water from this humble-looking river becoming part of the power and majesty of Niagara. She couldn't see her reflection in the river from this distance above it but might as well have. Wasn't she too ordinary, too unspectacular, to make much of a splash in this world too?

Her parents often reminded her, "The story you tell yourself is rarely the whole truth, Piper."

She watched another few thousand gallons make their way under the bridge and toward the cascade of wonder they were destined for.

When Elliott and Piper returned to the inn, they split the duties of laundering the Lumber Baron Suite's linens, replacing towels, and sanitizing everything that needed it. Piper had spent the time putting finishing touches on the room she'd been given. She might not be there long, but it could still feel more like home. No sense living out of a suitcase with that perfectly good antique armoire in the corner and the marble-topped, lavender-lined dresser.

She'd stopped to key in an online search for "moose and butterfly carving." She got a few hits of the garden gnome variety, but nothing like what she had seen in the photo from 1902. And nothing historical that traced back to a story she could use.

More reason to rest her hopes on a conversation with the chatty Mrs. Finster in the morning.

Elliott and Piper mutually agreed that a light supper was all they needed. Sandwiches and Grandma Peggy own preserved peaches from the pantry. They caught up on what they knew of mutual friends from college, challenges and joys of their chosen careers, and favorite books they'd read recently.

"I should take advantage of your grandmother's collection while I'm here," Piper had said, reaching for a well-worn volume in the glass-front bookcase in the parlor where they'd shared their after-dinner conversation.

"Please feel free," Elliott said. "She has a fascinating book about the Peshtigo fire. The fire had to have affected the timber industry here too."

His casually introduced idea had kept the flames of their conversation ablaze long into the night.

All she'd had to say was, "Tell me the story."

"You're probably familiar with the Great Chicago Fire, right?"

"Mrs. O'Leary's cow kicked over the lantern?"

Elliott smiled. "So say some. Devastated much of the city of Chicago. Fall of 1871."

Piper didn't mind listening to that caramel-smooth voice, but she did hope he would make the leap to something that connected to Embarrass, other than a cow's embarrassingly thorough ability to level a city.

"Same day, *same day* mind you, a fire swept through just north and east of here, near Peshtigo. It burned something like a million and a half acres and did almost as much financial damage as the Chicago fire. Hundreds of lives lost. The entire town of Peshtigo was leveled in an hour, the flames were so intense and fast-moving."

"Could that explain why so few historic buildings are still standing around here?"

"As far-reaching as it was, the Peshtigo fire didn't come this far south. And Embarrass was likely just a handful of houses or farms back then. Not even a village yet. But the practices that started the fire could have certainly instigated lesser but still damaging fires closer to home."

She lingered on the word *home* for a moment while he sipped on sparkling cider.

"Both expanding the railroad and the timber industry," he said, "necessitated lighting fires to burn leftover brush after clearing land. The smell of smoke was so prevalent that on the night of the Peshtigo fire, no one considered it alarming until it was too late."

"That much destruction? From a simple brush fire?"

"They say that some years, brush fires they set dove down into the peat, where they smoldered all winter long. The prior winter was so devoid of snow that kids reported seeing the ground glowing."

Piper bookmarked a website about the Peshtigo fire then set her phone aside. "So much information available to us with a simple swipe or search. Why is it so hard to dig up more about the history of this inn and the village? What I've gotten from the files Kelly shared hasn't been much more than dry statistics. This week, with your permission, I'll rummage through your grandmother's desk drawers."

"Have at it," Elliott said. "Oddly, the only thing Gram specifically mentioned we couldn't touch was that silly apron. I have a few more days of tight deadlines for work, then I'll be freer to help."

"And guests this week…?"

"Nothing on the books until Carlton returns the week after this one."

Carlton. Maybe Mrs. Finster could shed some light on that story too.

CHAPTER EIGHT

Piper intentionally arrived more than a half hour early for her lunch appointment with Mrs. Finster. Clintonville's Living Room Coffee Shop and Vintage Decor building looked like it might have been a gas station in a previous life. Still, it oozed charm. A feast for the eyes and the senses.

She purposefully dodged the mesmerizing aroma of "proper" coffee and baked goods and instead perused the displays of artwork, jewelry, furniture, and craft items for sale. Mostly local artisans with wares from an antique dealer thrown in here and there, according to signage.

The watercolors displayed in an antique step-back cupboard caught her eye. Such a delicate touch. The closer she drew, the more familiar they looked. Each seemed to be a melding of a historical site or property with a modern-day version of it. Just like the image of the inn. The paintings were unsigned. Unlabeled.

"Don't miss the back room," a young woman behind the counter called her way. "Lots more to see in there."

"Can you tell me anything about this artist?"

"I'm afraid not. The artist prefers to remain anonymous."

Piper would find out. But how? Mrs. Finster?

What Piper assumed was a small storefront building held much more behind the scenes. She scanned the back room with an eye for items she could use to add a little more color to her apartment, and for anything resembling a clue. Her latest searches for the history of Embarrass turned up embarrassingly slim results. In the late 1880s, a log dam had provided water pressure to run a sawmill, then a flour mill. That was it. An online search about how many holes there are in a whiffle ball would have netted her pages of information.

A whole village's history? Practically nothing.

But that couldn't be the end of the story.

Piper found quilted place mats she snatched up, just in case the quilters' retreat idea stuck. If not, she'd find some other use for them. Porcelain teapots. All shapes, sizes, and colors. A bonanza for the tearoom that didn't yet exist. Small silver teaspoons with words like *Hope, Peace, Joy,* and *Faith* engraved on the handles.

Elliott hadn't given her a budget for supplies. These might wind up as her personal property, or her gift to the inn, to the cause. But she could envision them adorning a decked-out parlor filled with happy, paying customers.

On a worn velvet loveseat near the front window, two older women were deep in conversation. A businessman and business-woman with dueling laptops occupied one of several mismatched tables. Another served as what looked like a crafting corner for a woman with a flair for all things bohemian…and knitting. She had no coffee, tea, or lunch in front of her. Socially unconventional?

Perhaps not as much as the heavyset gentleman in clothes that looked like they had been through a paint-shaker machine. He leaned back in his chair and tapped on the tabletop in front of him. At his feet rested a canvas bag. Piper could only imagine what it held. Maybe all his worldly goods.

"Heading back to the easel, Morton?" the barista asked.

"Pretty soon," the man said, then drained his mug.

An artist. I stand corrected. In her perusal of the shop, she'd seen paintings she'd admired signed with a Morton-like flourish signature. Not the mysterious unnamed artist she was searching for. First impressions weren't always accurate. Or rather, first assumptions.

"Piper?"

She turned at her name.

"I'm—"

"Mrs. Finster? So good to meet you."

"Likewise. Any friend of Elliott's…"

"I'm grateful you had time for me today."

"Have you ordered yet?" The woman's attention drifted to the chalkboard menus above the coffee machines.

"No. What do you recommend?"

"All of their sandwiches are good. This time of year, they have a larger selection of salads too. The Dairy State salad is exceptional."

Piper scanned the menus for salads. There it was. *Spring mix greens with dried cranberries, dried blueberries, smoked trout, and cheese curds, with apple cider vinaigrette.* A little out of the norm, but why not?

They placed their orders and looked for an open table.

They settled in across from one another.

"Do you mind if I take notes, Mrs. Finster?"

"For your article?"

"I'm not writing an… Well, that's not a bad idea. Thanks. You've been helpful already." A few carefully placed articles in online resources might help. Wisconsin must have a "Fun Things to Do in

Wisconsin" site. Titles scrolled across her brain. *Vacation Where No One Else Does. Boost Your Self-Confidence in Embarrass, Wisconsin. Main Street Inn—Where the Vacancy Sign is Always Lit.*

"Did your daughter get off okay?"

Mrs. Finster glanced around the room. Apparently satisfied all listening ears were otherwise engaged, she said, "Yes, she did. Thank you for asking." Her tone convinced Piper that was the last they'd discuss about the younger Finster.

"I hoped you'd be able to help me with research I'm conducting on the history and residents of Embarrass."

"What for?"

"I know there has to be a story here."

"I've lived in Embarrass my whole life, and I'm looking at sixty in my rearview mirror, so ask away."

No smile. The woman's face was a study in flatness, like the difference between matte and glossy lipstick. Her eyebrows moved up and down, mostly up. But nothing else seemed at all animated... until she suddenly brightened.

"Gloria! Great to see you." She waved at a younger, well-dressed woman entering the establishment. "I can't talk now. I'm being interviewed." She pointed at Piper.

Obligingly, Piper smiled and raised her notebook, as if Gloria needed proof.

Mrs. Finster once again gave her attention to Piper. The flat version returned. "You were saying?"

"Is your family from this area? Parents? Grandparents?"

"They're gone now."

"Did they have stories to tell about…anything of interest in Embarrass?"

"Not much to tell. Everybody minds their own business."

I'm sure they do. "Anything remarkable? I'm especially interested in the history of the inn, of course."

"I'm sure Peggy Lansing would be the person to ask."

"As you may know, she's—"

"Yes. Gallivanting to who knows where. At her age. Europe's not safe, you know."

Piper considered the recent news alerts about dangers on US soil, but she refrained from bringing them up. "I'm sure she's enjoying the art and architecture and the break from running the inn. I'd love to find information even she's not yet aware of. Surprise her."

"Not sure what I can offer. This whole area has its roots in the timber industry. And that's about it. There's a park here, I'm sure you've seen it, that is centered around the remains of the once-thriving lumber mill. Now it's mostly a place to gather for the Fireman's Picnic and such."

"Yes, I have that information. Do you know anything about the original owners of the inn? Or perhaps the second owners?"

"Not sure I was ever curious about that. I don't hear people talking about it. Why?"

Their salads and homemade lemonades arrived. Piper slid her notebook to the side and determined to show Mrs. Finster she was interested in her as a person while they ate.

"Do you have just one daughter, Mrs. Finster? Any other children?"

"Well, aren't you the nosy one."

"I apologize."

"That was my attempt at sarcasm."

"Oh."

"I have five daughters. One left to marry off."

"Sarcasm again?"

"I don't know what you mean by that."

Piper sipped on the tart but luscious lemonade and glanced at the knitter, who hadn't said a word to anyone as far as Piper could tell. But the woman might be more helpful than Piper's current lunch companion.

New idea. "Do you know Carlton—" What was his last name?

"Of course."

Piper had to be careful. She didn't dare divulge anything that the man didn't want shared. Maybe no one but she and Elliott and Gram knew he spent a night every other week at the inn. "I…met him."

"Did you now?"

"He doesn't talk much."

Mrs. Finster's eyebrows rose again, like a lift bridge of brows letting the seagoing vessels of her eyes pass underneath. "Is that a problem?"

"No. Not at all. I just wondered if you knew him. Or…anything about him."

"Seems to me that's his own business."

The way I heard it, you know everyone else's. Are you hoarding the juicy tidbits for yourself, Mrs. Finster? "You're right." Piper reined in her renegade commentary. "Any villagers you can think of who might have heard stories passed down from their"—she did the math in her head—"parents or grandparents?" If an Embarrasser was ninety, his parents may have been around when the hotel-now-an-inn was built. The *hotel* angle. Maybe she could add that search word to her online investigation.

"You could ask the garden club."

Piper almost choked on a dried cranberry. At last, her "interviewee" was volunteering information. "How wonderful that there's an active garden club in Embarrass."

"Don't know if you'd exactly call them *active*. Most are in their eighties or older."

"How often do they meet?"

Mrs. Finster glanced at her wristwatch. "Weekly, unless there's a bug going around."

"Oh. Of course. At their age, they would want to avoid the flu at all costs."

"Flu? Sure. I meant aphids, though. If they're fighting an infestation of aphids or potato beetles, you don't see much of the garden club ladies."

"Women only?"

"Technically, no. Ethel's ex-husband comes, but that's mostly because she can't drive. He shouldn't be driving, if you ask me. But he's a sight safer on the road that she would be."

"Ex-husband?"

"Those two are doing a lot better since the divorce. They probably could have just stayed married and taken separate bedrooms. But his snoring was an 'irreconcilable difference.'" She glanced at her watch again then looked up as the bell over the door jangled. "Here come the first of them now."

Piper would have described the Embarrass Garden Club as *marching* into the Clintonville establishment, but few armies marched that slowly, or noisily. They chattered like chickadees fighting for dominance at a bird feeder. Happy chatter, for the most part. A man Piper assumed was the ex-husband held the door for the others then took the elbow of a woman she sincerely hoped was Ethel.

Mrs. Finster introduced her to them all. Who *was* this enigmatic woman? One moment closed up tight and the next emceeing the meet and greet?

Piper got busy scribbling notes. Most of the "remember whens" held value only to the storytellers, but somewhere in there she might find a nugget that could lead to the mother lode she was desperate to find.

Elliott weighed his options. He'd created and deleted three text messages to Piper already. If there was any doubt he'd hired the right woman, it had long since faded. She brought so much more than expertise to this inn-saving project.

Joy? That was part of it. Exuberance? Definitely. Dogged determination? Yes. But more.

As the thought began to form in his mind, he considered resisting it but stopped himself from doing so. His life was better with her in it. It had been true during their college days, though he'd never dared to express it.

Was it time to admit to himself that he hoped for more than a few weeks working side by side with her? Time to admit it to her? No.

And his latest find might shorten their time together. It could lead to an answer, which would lead to Piper returning to her real life, not this temporary gig.

But he had to at least tell her about what he'd discovered.

Didn't he?

He set his phone aside. The news could wait until she got back.

∽ CHAPTER NINE ∾

Which smelled sweeter—the spring air or the woman riding it as she breezed into the kitchen through the back hall? And tripped on the raised threshold. She winced, steadied herself on the doorjamb, shook her foot as if trying to free herself from something stuck to the bottom of it, and then kept breezing.

"Elliott! So glad you're not involved in something. I have a great idea!"

His news could wait a little longer. "What is it this time?"

"*Save the Inn...Save the Village.*" She deposited her purse and a shopping bag on the table. "I've been talking to the garden club."

"How did you get connected to the garden club?"

"Mrs. Finster introduced me."

"Mrs. Finster?"

"Long story. Do you want to hear my idea or not?"

"Of course." Elliott extended his coffee mug to her and pointed from it to Piper to ask if she wanted some.

"Would love it. Thanks. So, here's my idea. We get the whole town involved in this. We need to help them see that if we revitalize the inn, the whole town benefits. All the businesses..."

"All two of them."

"Elliott."

"Under-exaggeration."

"We can do a big campaign with yard signs and maybe a fund-raising element, and I'll write articles for area news outlets, or maybe even statewide. Instead of trying to squeeze information out of the townspeople, most who are too young to—"

"Did you say too *young?*"

"Younger than a hundred and twenty. Anyway, too young to have personal memories about what this inn and the village were like at their beginnings in the late 1800s. Without much recorded history, we're left with having to rely on stories passed from one generation to another. And so far, that hasn't amounted to much. Most of it sounds like an unsuccessful game of telephone."

"You've only been here a few days."

"But we don't have a lot of time."

I was just thinking that a few minutes ago. "So, your plan…"

"…includes a contest to rename the inn." She clapped her hands together before accepting the coffee mug he offered. "What do people in small towns love to do more than anything?"

"Plant gardens?"

"No. Well, yes. And that could factor in here, but they love to share their opinions."

"Doesn't that pretty much describe society as a whole?"

"Elliott, can we stick to the plan?"

"Yes. I'm all ears." Except he wasn't. His heart was making its presence known.

"A contest to rename the inn."

Elliott sighed. He might already have the name, if it came with enough of a backstory.

"Or," she said, "a tagline that links the town and the inn. Something like 'Who wouldn't want to land in the heart of Embarrass?' That might need some work. What do you think?"

"Yes. It needs some work."

"See? Everyone has an opinion. What do you think about the *Save the Inn...Save the Village* concept?"

"Do the townspeople think the village needs saving?"

She took two steps and bent at the waist. "Ow."

"Did that offend you? I didn't mean..."

"Ow, ow, ow." She leaned on the table.

"Piper, seriously. It was just a question."

"Elliott. I'm not offended. I stepped off the curb funny at the restaurant after my conversation with the garden club. Not uncommon for me. I thought it was okay. Now I'm not so sure. Something popped when I tripped over the threshold. Did you hear that?" She lowered herself into a kitchen chair, lifted her leg, and propped the offended foot on another chair.

"Are you okay?"

"Pretty sure I'm not. This isn't going to work." She lowered her foot back to the ground. "Remember how accident prone I was in college?"

He did. And how much he'd wanted to be her rescuer.

"Seems I haven't grown out of that. Left ankle? Freshman year. Right ankle? Junior year. This feels like junior year."

Elliott knelt at her feet. "May I?"

"May you what?"

"See if it looks broken?"

"Yes, please. But I'm not a broken bones kind of klutzy. I'm more of a bruised, twisted, and sprained kind of gal."

She winced when he cupped her heel in one hand.

"Relax, if you can. I'll be gentle."

He removed her tennis shoe and studied her ankle, then lifted the other to compare them side by side.

"Well, Dr. Elliott?"

"Is that a subtle reminder of how different my life would be if I'd continued to pursue premed?"

She flicked him on the head. "It's a reference to your ability to tell me what seems obvious. This one is definitely swollen. Ugh. I don't like being slowed down, as you may have noticed."

"Let's get you to a doctor."

"I know how this goes. Lots of practice. Ice it right away and elevate the thing. If I don't overdo it, it'll be better in a few days."

"And if not?"

"Then I'll let you take me to a doctor."

"Do you need something for pain?" Why was it he felt her distress in his gut?

"Yes. Do we have any cheesecake left? I skipped dessert at the restaurant."

Elliott couldn't help but laugh.

He set her up with a pillow for her ankle and ice to reduce the swelling then supplied her with the only pain med she said she needed.

But he was sitting on information that might provide relief too. When she seemed more comfortable and about to open her laptop, he interjected, "I found something of interest."

"What?" She leaned forward, as he suspected she would.

He crossed to the corner and closed the previously open door to the back hall. "This." He pointed to the apron.

"What about it?" She gasped. "You didn't...touch it, did you? After your grandmother's warning?"

Elliott quirked an eyebrow. "She was specifically talking about *you* wearing it, I believe. She didn't mention...*specifically*...that *I* couldn't touch it."

Piper squinted. "Elliott."

"Do you want to know what I discovered or not?"

"Absolutely! Spill the tea!"

He picked the apron off its hook with two fingers and carried it to where she sat. "What do you see?"

"Old fabric. Two ties for the waist. Two pockets."

"Yes. Pockets."

"Elliott, did you dig around in the pockets of the apron Grandma Peggy said to not ever under any circumstances mess with?"

"Guilty as charged. But I didn't exactly *dig* in them, and she was, again, talking about you."

"Where is it?"

"What?"

"Whatever it was you found in one of the pockets?"

"They were empty."

The disappointment on her face pushed him forward. "Technically, they were empty. Have a look." He pulled one pocket open as if peeling back a piece of fragile parchment.

"Empty, all right," she said.

"Look again, in this general area."

She gasped again. "Oh, Elliott!"

"That's hand-embroidered, isn't it? I don't know if you call that a cuff of a pocket or what, but that clearly says—"

"'The Moose and Butterfly Inn.'" Her eyes met his.

"Same beautiful embroidering in the other pocket."

"Does your grandmother embroider?"

"Not that I know of."

"Was this what she didn't want us to see? And why would she have felt it important to keep it from us?"

"Good questions. I think it may be time for us to interrupt her adventure to get some answers." He pulled out his phone.

"Elliott. Wait."

"She has to know something."

"But she might also have a reason for us not to discover it."

"Which puts us in an awkward place if tasked with making all this work." He gestured as if encompassing the entire, many-storied building.

"Let's think for a minute. Longer than a minute. It's past her bedtime in Italy or wherever she and her friend are today."

"A point worth considering."

"And another thing."

Elliott rehung the apron. "What's that?"

"Cheesecake isn't the high-powered painkiller I thought it would be."

"You need some ibuprofen?"

"Please. And…"

"A comfier chair?"

"You read my mind."

I'm reduced to this, am I? Piper used a chopstick to scratch a spot under the black, clunky walking boot. "Aircast, my foot."

"I see what you did there," Elliott said. "My foot?"

"Feels more like a boat anchor."

"Can I get you something? Perhaps a mood-brightening cup of tea? Or a whole teapot full?"

"Am I a bad patient?"

"Noooo," Elliot said, drawing out the o's like someone born in Wisconsin.

"Thanks for hauling me to Urgent Care yesterday. And for sitting with me the whole time. And for hauling me home. And for all you're doing."

"I didn't consider it 'hauling.' More like accompanying you on a healing journey."

"You read that in a book, didn't you?" She hadn't minded extra time with him and certainly didn't mind his extra attentiveness. But she had things to do, places to go. She didn't need a fancy black plastic-and-Velcro anchor weighing her down. Talk about bad timing. Although, when would have been *good* timing to sprain her ankle with a possible hairline fracture?

"I can never have children," she said.

"What?" Elliott looked stricken.

"Can you imagine having a mother with this propensity for minor injuries?"

Elliott's expression changed from stricken to sober. "I had a mother prone to emotional sprains. I know which is worse."

"I can never quit my job," she said. "I need the extra-strength health insurance."

He chuckled and headed for the kitchen, leaving her alone in the cozy parlor, on the plush fainting couch—how fitting. Seconds later he popped his head into the room.

"Iced or hot?"

"I've had enough icing my ankle for a while, and it's too warm today for a hot pack."

"Your tea, Piper?"

"Oh. Iced. I don't remember answering whether I wanted any."

"I don't remember you ever turning down tea."

He was gone again.

Being with Elliott was bringing back feelings she hadn't known since college. She'd written him out of her life. Now here he was again, albeit temporarily. Her wonderings came out in a prayer. *God, how am I supposed to feel? What am I supposed to do?*

"Enjoy."

That was quick, Lord. Oh. Elliott was back with the tea. "Thanks so much."

"Do you want to talk business or not?"

I want to enjoy. But her business and Elliott Lansing were inextricably entwined these days, so enjoy she would. "What's on your mind?"

"I like your idea of changing the name back to the Moose and Butterfly Inn."

"Great." She sat up a little straighter.

"But two things stand in the way. We'd have to clear it with Gram."

"Of course."

"And we need to know the real story. In case the original Moose and Butterfly was a—you know—something less than respectable."

"Elliott! It can't have been."

"How do we know?"

"Look at that young couple in the photograph. The Moose guy and the Butterfly-like woman. There's innocence written all over their faces."

"Is that what you see?"

"I think anyone would. The storyline's all mapped out in my head. He was hunting moose one day and found her chasing butterflies in a meadow—"

"They didn't have much in the way of meadows around here at the end of the 1800s. It was either timberland or land that had been stripped of the timber. Stumpy, rough terrain or a few fields that had been cleared of stumps for wheat farming."

"I can change that. He found her chasing butterflies in a forest and—"

"Sounds too much like Little Red Riding Hood."

"I'm used to enhancing a story to fit our marketing needs. Let's see. He's hunting moose and sees a butterfly. It reminds him of the schoolmarm…"

"Piper."

"So he catches it and puts it in his pocket and takes it back to the village with him. When he gets to the school building, he sees billowing smoke and rushes through the flames to save her."

"Just her? What about the children?"

Piper shifted, cringed, then continued. "It was a snow day."

"With butterflies?"

"Right. Not believable."

"None of it is." Elliott hummed something. Oh no. He was clearing his throat for whatever he intended to say next.

"It can't be fake. Misleading. Smarmy."

"Did you just use the word *smarmy?*"

"It can't be fiction, Piper."

"The best fiction is based on truth," she said.

"But if one day the real story of this Moose and Butterfly is discovered and it's scandalous or…"

"Smarmy."

"Right. Talk about bad PR."

"At the moment we have *no* PR and the potential of creating some."

"We need to keep looking for the authentic, Piper. And get Gram's approval first."

Piper exhaled as if trying to extinguish a candle, which led to a light bulb dancing in her imagination above her head. "Maybe not first."

Elliott rested his chin in his hand. "What are you thinking?"

"If we uncover who those people really were and how utterly wonderful…"

"If they were."

"Their story might just be what convinces Gram to consider the name change. And that starts the ball rolling with all that's been on hold—the website, the advertising, events…" She swung her legs around, tightened her core muscles, and stood without assistance. "I have an idea."

"Oh, here we go."

She planted a hand on her hip. "Elliott, did you know that Mrs. Finster is not fluent in sarcasm?"

"No."

"And neither are you." She exited the room before he could say more.

∽ CHAPTER TEN ∾

The Garden Club apparently knew how to dig dirt in more ways than one.

"You need to talk to Arlene Cornell," one of them had said during their prolonged visit at the Living Room Coffee Shop and Vintage Decor. "She used to be the librarian. She's sure to have something."

On day three of Piper's recuperation, a woman unexpectedly showed up at the front door of the inn. Correction. On the sidewalk in front of the inn. Staring. Unmoving. Piper wouldn't have known she was there if she hadn't decided to sit on the front porch to work that morning.

"May I help you?" she asked.

"Arlene Cornell."

"What a pleasure to meet you. I've heard so much about you."

The woman didn't move, although she had to have noticed Piper's anchor-like boot.

"Come join me on the porch," Piper said.

"No, thank you. No."

"It's a little awkward to chat with this much distance between us." Piper eyed the woman's pinched expression that matched the pinched look of her clothes. She oozed discomfort, evidenced in part by the way she fiddled with the necklace she wore.

"I'm not here to chat. I'm here to tell you to stop this nonsense about investigating the history of the...this inn or whatever you're calling it."

"Stop? Why?"

The woman considered for a moment. "Because I'm asking you to, that's why."

"We don't even know each other, Ms. Cornell." Piper mentally dialed down the volume and intensity of what she wanted to say to the woman. "I have only good intentions at heart."

The woman raised her chin. "Good intentions can be just as destructive as no intentions at all."

Piper stood and, holding the post near the steps, hobbled down one, then another, until she was on level ground with Arlene Cornell. "Please come in so we can talk. I wouldn't want anything I'm doing to cause trouble for Embarrass."

Arlene huffed. "Some things are better left untouched, and that's all I'm going to say."

"Can I offer you coffee or tea or—"

"I've been standing here long enough. Too long. Just leave it be. I'm asking nice. This time."

The woman turned on her rubber-soled shoes and crossed the street, not once looking back as she hightailed it out of speaking distance.

What was that all about? *Lord, please don't let Elliott's suspicions be right, that there's an unsavory story connected to his grandmother's business.*

The woman's words had a sinister air to them. Not what they needed. Not in the least.

She hobbled back up the steps, trembling more than she'd realized, and retreated inside. Maybe it was a day to scour the place for ledgers or bookkeeping files or ancient records of the inn's reservations. Paper records like that might be stored in the attic.

Elliott was recording. She'd have to be quiet. Her pirate gait—step THUMP, step THUMP—wasn't going to help. Hopping on one leg would be even worse. She'd have to ease herself up the attic stairway on her behind.

After maneuvering the challenging enough well-carpeted steps to the second floor, she did a modified version of tiptoeing to the narrow door Elliott had told her led to the attic. Unlocked. She opened it slowly. At the first "creak" she'd be discovered on a mission she wasn't convinced Elliott would approve of, considering her extra footwear.

Good news. The layers of dust on the rustic stairs might help dampen sound.

Once seated on the bottom step, she pulled the door closed. A second later, she tapped the flashlight feature on her phone and tucked it into her shirt pocket. An eerie light for detective work, but she wasn't about to interrupt Elliott at all, much less ask him where to find a larger flashlight.

What she hadn't calculated was how she'd stand once she reached the top step. The muscles in her right leg ached from holding her booted ankle straight out to keep it from bumping the steps or the side walls. Her hands were filthy. But all that was of far less consequence than her inability to get herself upright from the floor without assistance or support.

She turned her torso. Her pocket illuminated an enormous attic. Not unexpectedly, it was like a museum of this-n-that. If she could wiggle herself, still sitting, as far as that old desk, she might be able to use it to pull herself to standing.

Elliott's studio wasn't far beneath her. She could only hope his headphones were noise-canceling. She listened for his deep, soul-stirring voice. Nothing. That meant he was either on a break or the soundproofing he'd rigged up was working.

It wasn't pretty, but she managed to stand without clunking anything. Where should she start?

Something brushed the top of her head. She stifled a scream and reached up to slap the object, critter, or cobweb away. A string. A pull-cord for a light bulb dangled from the ceiling. Great place to begin.

Even though the attic was full, it wasn't disorderly or chaotic. *Way to go, Grandma Peggy.* It would help that Piper wouldn't have to dig through unknown piles of scary stuff.

What if—

Even with light from the single bulb, she needed her phone flashlight to scan the far corners. What if she stumbled onto the wood carving of the moose with the butterfly on its nose? Wouldn't that be glorious? They could probably find a chainsaw-happy modern lumberjack person who could create a duplicate from the old photograph, but Elliott was right. It had to be authentic, or what was the point?

Nothing in the attic looked remotely the size and shape of what she'd seen in the picture. She couldn't imagine any of the trunks or boxes were large enough. What was she thinking? It was likely long gone. Used for firewood. Sold to a resale shop.

All the options seemed equally awful to her. Something about that image and that young couple had captured her heart.

Her phone pinged. Why hadn't she silenced it? A text from Elliott.

Done recording in about an hour. Little editing yet. Short road trip?

With the phone now silenced and unable to ping again, she typed, Where to?

Logging camp.

An attic full of possibilities awaited her. She had less than an hour to gather as much intel as she could. And then slap on a "Sure, I'd love to go to a logging camp" face. Right after she crawled down the narrow stairs and changed out of her dust-encrusted clothes.

Love to, she responded. Not because of logs and a camp and lumberjacks. But because of the guy with the velvet voice.

Less than an hour. She'd take pictures of whatever she found interesting and study them later. Get the images captured. Worry about contents and significance afterward. Just like all good spies.

Only a few feet into her search, she discovered a gold mine of information. Boxed by years or decades, a wealth of info was there for the taking, or rather digitally photographing. She paged through saved images of registered guests, billing for equipment and supplies and food purchases, and tax records kept way longer than legally necessary.

It didn't take long to find what she hoped would glean the most relevant yet oldest information. The earliest formal recordkeeping she could find traced all the way back to the late 1800s when it was called the Galloway Hotel. Grave disappointment. That much Elliott suspected already.

As fast as she dared go without making noise, she thumbed through page after page of information with one eye on the time.

And there it was. The name change. The first of them, at least. *The Moose and Butterfly Inn. Established 1902. Owners Élan and Lilly Lamoreaux.*

Tucked into pages listing expenses was a yellowed flyer announcing the Grand Opening. On the front of the four-page flyer was an ink etching of the moose/butterfly carving. She turned to the interior. A two-page, elegantly lettered menu for the Grand Opening. And on the back page, "A Short History."

She should just take a picture of each page and keep searching. But the history irresistibly drew her attention. Too rich. Too good. More than she imagined.

How could she leave it there in the attic? She tucked it inside her shirt and continued her search through the decades. When did the name change yet again? Guest registers. Payroll. *Ah!*

Her fingers trembled as she focused the camera lens on the time-worn wages page. A groundskeeper had been hired to manage the property in the late 1940s—a man named Howard Cornell. Also listed was a son, Howard Jr., who was paid for lawn care.

Piper calculated the years. If she was right, Howard Jr. might be Arlene's husband.

There had to be more. But she needed time to exit the attic before Elliott emerged from his studio. Evidence first. Then she'd explain her actions.

Five more minutes. How much could she absorb in that little time? Enough.

An envelope stuck between two ledgers slid to the floor. In it, there were three small French coins and a note that said, *As I move on to my next adventure, I give you all I have to my name. These three coins, and the pin that showed I was once honored by my mentor, as I now honor you. Merci.* It was signed *Jean-Claude Pascal.* Why did that sound so familiar? Oh! The menu for the Grand Opening.

The entrée bore his name.

Relieved to have accomplished so much, Elliott exited his studio room and nearly ran into a freshly showered Piper. Cheeks flushed. Hair damp. She'd either been lifting weights or... No, she smelled like lavender.

"You didn't have to change for our road trip," he said, noting her short-sleeved sundress.

"It seemed like a good idea." Piper shrugged.

"Grab a jacket or sweater though."

"How far away is this logging camp? Canada? The North Pole?"

"Shawano. But the weather around here can change quickly, as you've probably noticed."

"Got it. Give me a few minutes to dry my hair?"

Elliott stopped the "sure" from leaving his mouth and instead said, "I could rustle you up a beaver skin ear-flap hat."

Without missing a beat, she said, "Save that for winter."

Winter. When she'd be gone from his life again. When the inn itself might be missing in action or taken over by a bank with no heart connection to it.

He never liked winter.

He should have thought through what uneven ground at the lumber camp museum would do to a woman in a walking boot. Wrongly, he'd imagined smooth sidewalks between the historical log buildings.

She could have opted to remain in the modern building that housed the gift shop, video presentations, and public restrooms, plus several comfortable couches. But Piper's FOMA—fear of missing *anything*—won out.

She said it helped if she had his arm to lean on. It was the least he could do.

They took their time wandering the grounds and the structures, viewing antique logging and milling machinery and equipment.

Piper seemed only mildly interested in the rusted equipment, although she did express her fascination with the loggers' innovations and creativity.

It was the bunkhouse and cook's shanty that captured her attention. His too. The array of hand tools, the barebones rough conditions the loggers worked and slept in, and the carvings and photographic images hanging on the walls vividly depicted life at camp, on the river, with loggers risking their lives atop sky-high log jams.

Elliott studied the broad axes, cant hooks, cross-cut saws, and sharp pickaroons while Piper got as close as she could to the photographs. Hundreds of them lined the walls. Two groups of elementary-aged children on a mid-May field trip swept through around them, but Elliott was content to let Piper linger as long as she wanted. She seemed intent on the faces of the loggers and the captions under the images.

What made him look up a moment before she stumbled backward? He scrambled to where she was and caught her as her bad leg slid sideways.

"You okay, Piper?"

"Thanks for the save. Staying upright isn't my strongest skillset."

"We can both agree there."

"But investigation is." She took a breath and straightened her posture. Her face seemed radiant.

"Look at that." She hobbled closer to the wall again and rested her finger under the chin of a burly logger.

"Good-looking guy. I wonder if he works out."

"Very funny, Elliott. Does the face seem familiar?" She traced her finger down the glass of the frame to the names at the bottom. "Row three, fourth from the left. I give you Élan—Moose—Lamoreaux."

"Our Moose?"

"The one and only."

Elliott squinted at the image. "It looks as if a lot of these men could have had the nickname Moose."

Piper tapped on the glass then withdrew her hand when a museum docent entered with another band of schoolchildren. "But," she whispered, "none with the first name Élan, which means 'moose' in French, which I almost remembered from high school French but did have to look it up, and the last name Lamoreaux."

Elliott keyed the name Lamoreaux into his phone and hit Search. "'The loving one, the amorous one'? Moose Love?" he whispered back.

"Do you know your grandmother's mother's maiden name, Elliott?"

"No. It never came up in conversation."

"I do. Research. Lamoreaux."

Elliott scratched his jawline. "Could be coincidence, couldn't it?" Even as he said it, he knew that a shared name like that was a mighty curious coincidence. "Grandma Peggy's mom was a Lamoreaux? I thought the inn had been passed down through my grandfather's line."

"Come back to the cook's shanty with me," she said.

"Why?"

"We're collecting puzzle pieces."

They made their way out of the log bunkhouse to the nearby shanty, a replica of the original that, according to signage, had long since decayed. He followed Piper across the wood plank floor to a display of cookware.

"Who does that look like to you, Elliott?" She swept her hand toward yet another photograph as if introducing him to a new model of car.

"In the background? It's a woman."

"Yes."

"Highly unusual for a lumber camp, I would imagine."

"Right again."

"That's not…"

She tilted her head and caught his gaze. Her eyebrows said, "Or is it?"

"The Butterfly?"

"If not," Piper said, "it's her twin sister. The resemblance is so strong to the woman in the watercolor dual-time painting of the inn."

He'd thought the trip to the lumber camp museum might give them insights about the logging industry, not puzzle pieces about the inn's history. "Are you certain this is the same woman? These artifacts have been gathered from many different camps in the area, not just this location."

"And yet," she said, "we found both of them here. The Moose. And the Butterfly. Lilly."

"Her name was Lilly?"

"Well, I assume so, since the other name in the caption is Jean-Claude Pascal, and the dude with the chef's hat and the rolling pin looks a lot more like a Jean-Claude than a Lilly."

He needed a minute.

"You're processing, aren't you?" Piper said.

"Little bit."

"It's a lot to take in. But trust me, there's more. Back home."

"And by *home* you mean…"

"The inn. I discovered a few things that will help this make sense."

"Where?"

Her eyes grew wide with feigned innocence and silence.

He extended his arm for her to lean on as they made their way to the car. "Do we have all the puzzle pieces we need now, in your expert opinion, Detective Merrill?"

"Far from it. Lots of dangling threads to untangle. But we're making real progress at last."

She was. In his mind, the dangling threads were more tangled than ever.

CHAPTER ELEVEN

"The attic? You went up to the attic alone?" Elliott's glance heavenward was either a consideration of the attic two stories above where they sat, a prayer, or an eye roll. Piper couldn't be sure.

"It's not that I'm completely crippled. I'm still alive, as you'll notice."

"I think you've mistaken me for someone else." Elliott hung his head like a petulant child.

"Someone else? Someone who cares about my safety but recognizes that I'm perfectly capable of making wise decisions?"

"No," Elliott said. "I *am* that guy."

"Oh."

"You mistook me for someone who doesn't trust you."

Not at all what she expected. "Thanks. You may not have appreciated the method I used to get up there though."

"Should I ask?"

"Please don't."

"Then I won't. I do admit I'm a little jealous."

"Of who?"

"Of what. I've been itching to get up there and snoop around. You beat me to it. I would love to have shared that experience with you."

Piper paused to let her heart rate slow. "There's plenty more up there to investigate."

"Good. After supper?"

"Not in a million years. An attic is iffy territory for me in broad daylight. I'm not keen on attics after dark, when—you know—bats take flight."

Elliott opened his mouth, closed it, then opened it again. "Bats come *out* of attics at night to take care of the mosquito population."

"You do know that means I'm never sitting around a backyard campfire again."

"I figured."

Piper took up her position on the fainting couch and loosened the Velcro on her walking cast.

"I'll be right back," Elliott said.

She decided to use the time to check the analytics on the inn's website. Any improvements since the minor updates she'd been able to make? Nothing noticeable. But there were two comments. From what Elliott said, that was rare.

Elliott returned with a heated therapy pad in one hand and an icy gel pack in the other. "Take your pick."

"You're spoiling me."

"Caring and spoiling are miles apart," he said, positioning the ice pack she'd pointed to over the splayed-open walking cast. He caught her gaze and held it for way too many heartbeats. "Miles."

A word like that from any other voice wouldn't have done what his version did to her. She either had to finish her job and leave this place soon, or she and her heart would have to do some heavy recovery work. He was flawlessly kind, but that was who Elliott was with everyone. It didn't necessarily mean what her heart was arguing it might. She'd been disappointed before.

She'd have to be careful.

'Tis better to have loved and lost than never to have loved at all.

"Get away from me!"

Elliott recoiled.

Oh no. I said that aloud. "I didn't mean you, Elliott. It was a thought. A fleeting thought." She laid her hand on his. "I'd never mean you. That is, I… It was a random thought I was attempting to brush away."

"You're getting tired of this sprained-maybe-busted ankle thing, aren't you?" His face had returned to its ever-compassionate mode.

"Y-yes. That's it. I am. I'll be so glad when I can ditch this encumbrance." She tapped the black contraption and winced.

"It probably wasn't a good idea for me to require so much walking of you at the museum."

"So worth it." She shifted perspectives. "My leg is tired, but my mind is whirling with the possibilities of what we discovered."

"Something interesting on your phone too?"

"I checked the website. We have a few comments."

Elliott's eyes widened.

"The first is a review from our second honeymoon couple."

"A good one, I hope?"

She turned the phone screen so he could see. He leaned closer from his perch at the end of the chaise.

"Nice. That can't hurt. But…can I have your phone for a second?"

"Sure."

He scrolled then frowned at the screen.

"What is it? Elliott? Let me see." His hesitation deepened her curiosity. "What's wrong? A spammer?"

"Not exactly." He returned her phone.

What she read turned her stomach, not in fear but anger. "Who would write something like that?"

"We can opt not to accept the comment. No one else will see it." Elliott slid a little closer on the chaise, noticeably careful of her propped leg.

"That's not the point. Someone's trying to stop us. Threatening us. Why? Who would have gone to the trouble to contact us through the website to say, 'Give it up. Your nosing around is going to end up in a world of hurt'?"

"I don't want to be intimidated by anyone, but…"

"We can't let this intimidate us, Elliott. Too much is at stake."

"Why the website? It's been practically dormant for the past few years."

Piper pressed her lips together.

"Do you know?"

"I posted an image of the carving with the caption, 'Stay tuned for more coming soon.' A teaser to let any web visitors know it wasn't a stagnant site. If your grandmother doesn't allow us to change the name, it'll still make a good story to include in the inn's history. How could that have stirred anything negative?"

"Good question."

"'A world of hurt.' That can't mean we're targets, can it? Like, real danger? That's ridiculous. The carving was part of the inn's history more than a hundred years ago. Who would care that much now? And why would it be a problem?"

Elliott stood and paced. "I don't want to worry Gram, and I sure don't want to interrupt the one stress-free time she's had in years, maybe ever."

"I don't either. This comment isn't enough to involve the police, is it?"

"We're not even sure it isn't as simple as a computer-generated hacker's work."

"Except…"

Elliott stopped pacing. "Except for what?"

"Arlene Cornell. Before my adventure in the attic, I was working on the front porch. A woman came partway up the sidewalk, introduced herself as Arlene Cornell, and in essence told me to 'Stop this nonsense about investigating the history of the inn.' I assumed she'd heard about what we're doing from the garden club. Honestly, I chalked it up to a cranky elderly woman who didn't appreciate an 'outsider' like me invading Embarrass territory."

"Arlene Cornell."

"You know her?"

"No, but I haven't gotten to know everyone in Embarrass. Older woman, you said?"

"And kind of intense, if you know what I mean. But then…" Now was the time. "Then I saw the name Cornell in the records in the attic. A Howard Cornell used to be a caretaker for the inn many years ago. And his son Howard Jr. did odd jobs here too."

"Cornell isn't an unusual name. It might not be connected."

"But it is."

"What?"

Piper braced herself on the fainting couch edges and sat upright. "I looked her up online. The Arlene Cornell I met, currently living in Embarrass, Wisconsin, is married to Howard Jr."

"What kind of vested interest might she have in keeping us from uncovering what happened here?"

"That's what I'd like to know. And there's only one way to find out." She set the ice pack aside and tightened her walking cast.

"Find Arlene and talk to her," Elliott suggested.

"To the attic!"

Piper's words had overlapped his. She had to plead her case. "Elliott, don't you think digging deeper into the attic will help us be better prepared for a conversation with Arlene?"

"Point well taken," he said. "Are you up to it?"

"If I let a twisted ankle—"

"Or broken."

"—or hairline fracture keep me from the excitement of discovery, I'd never get anything done."

"Also point well taken. If you're willing, let's head to the attic then. If you don't mind my offering my assistance for your ascent and descent."

"Much appreciated." *If I can keep my emotions in check.*

How would Elliott keep his emotions in check? Her nearness. Her exuberance. Her courage. When he'd hired Piper, he'd been confident he could manage all that, could stay focused on their business relationship. It was getting harder and harder to remain on task and ignore the whispers in his heart.

The shouts.

Obviously, more was at stake now than strengthening the inn's marketing and making it a profitable venture. As he helped Piper up the stairs, he realized he'd worried about all of what was going on, including in his crazy heart, far more than he had consulted the God his grandmother had taught him was always there, for any need.

Time to change that.

"I can't imagine you managing these narrow stairs on your own, Piper."

"A step at a time. Like anything else in life." She grunted with the effort to make the final rise. "There. Conquered. Now, let's go digging."

He followed as she *thunked* her way across the bare attic floor-boards to a spot with her fingerprints all over it. Literally. "You'd make a horrible spy, Piper. You don't cover your tracks well."

"I was in a bit of a hurry. Plus… No, that's it. I was in a hurry. I'll show you the photos I took of what I unearthed so far. It'll be easier to make out what they are if you view them on my laptop. But I didn't get any further than this. If we start here and move closer to the current day, we might find more clues."

"Grocery receipts?"

"You'd be amazed what pops up in the ordinary. That's how I found out Howard Cornell and his son were on the payroll. Then abruptly his name no longer appears in the records. And apparently, Howard was a single dad. He and his son lived on the property in a carriage house. From the records, it sounds like it stood where that old storage shed is out back now."

"When did Howard Cornell work here?" Elliott bent his tall frame over the ledger, but his body threw shadows on the pages in front of him. "Should we carry all this downstairs to examine? That single bulb isn't shedding much light."

Piper stood back and threw her arms wide. "Look at all these records. That's a lot to carry up and down."

"We could turn one of the guest rooms into a Situation Room. It's doubtful the Lumber Baron's Suite will be rented out again any time soon. It has room enough for us to set up folding tables and get you a comfortable chair. We can spread out the records by category or year."

"Or decade."

"Right."

Something skittered in the corner. Not unexpected in an establishment more than one hundred years old. And in an attic which grew warmer and stuffier by the minute. It could be Harvey the squirrel.

Piper made eye contact. "Downstairs. Great idea."

"Mark which boxes and books you think we'll want to look through first. I'll take care of transporting them, in light of—" He glanced at her boot.

"Sounds good to me. I didn't bring a pen. How will I mark them?"

He took her hand in his and pressed it on top of a dusty box as if fingerprinting her. "There you go."

"Brilliant, Mr. Holmes."

"Thank you, Dr. Watson."

Within the hour, the Situation Room hummed with activity. Piper had a gift for organizing, which he already knew. But it struck Elliott that he'd rarely seen such zest for life paired with the kind of practical, logical, responsible giftings he saw in this woman. He could only be grateful to have her there.

"I commend You for Your fine work," he said quietly.

Piper looked up. "Thanks, but I've barely started."

He wasn't obligated to tell her it was a prayer.

"I brought this down too," he said, placing a padlocked metal box on the last blank tabletop. "It seemed to scream, 'Look inside.'"

"We're going to have to pay Laverne more for all the extra dust we're making."

"Noted."

Piper made an official palm print on the top of the metal box then ran her fingers over the padlock. "A padlock seems to denote importance, don't you think? Let's start here. How good are you at lock picking?"

"Out of practice," he said. "But the dollar store sells replacement padlocks in case we should accidentally damage this one."

"I like how you think. Plan in place. Elliott?"

"Hmm?" He slid a straightened paper clip into the lock. Not the answer.

"Didn't you ever wonder if your grandmother might want to pass the inn on to you when she—when she no longer wants to run it?"

"Like an inheritance? She's convinced I wouldn't want it."

"Why?"

"Because I told her I wouldn't." He pulled a small pocketknife from his jeans and tried the multitool blade. Also not the answer.

Piper flipped through several pages before asking, "Do you still feel that way?"

He stopped messing with the lock and sat in the straight-backed chair he'd hauled from the kitchen. "That I *wouldn't* want it? No. I...I wouldn't want to tackle this *alone*. But despite its current lack of business and therefore income, there's something special about this place. Just...not...on my own."

She held his gaze a moment then turned back to the stacks of history on the tables. "Understood."

Is it? Do you understand I mean not without you, Piper? The place felt like an albatross until you crossed its threshold. Now it has... Oh, that was weird. The words that came to his mind were *butterfly wings.*

∽ CHAPTER TWELVE ∾

Was it encouraging or creepy that Piper had mad locksmith skills too? And the lock remained intact, so they could relock it without having to scour a rash of antique stores to find one like it.

"Ready to see what's inside?" she asked, hand poised on the lid.

"Your best guess?"

"A will or something. Deed to the property. War bonds."

"Which war?"

"Does it matter? Or maybe it's gold bars or—"

"It would be heavier."

She huffed. "Spoilsport."

"Let's just open it and find out. And we're committed that if it's terribly personal, Gram will never know."

Piper chewed her bottom lip. "I don't think I can commit to that, Elliott. You've been teaching me that a real story—however hard or awkward—is always better than a made-up one."

"True."

"We're going to have to confess."

"Okay. Agreed."

She lifted the lid. "Unless there's a secret compartment in this thing, this is no treasure."

"Old newspaper clippings."

"They're not in chronological order. I wonder why not?"

"'Hotel Owners Implicated As Accessories in Aiding and Abetting Suspected Jewel Thief.'"

"What? No! Not the Moose and Butterfly couple. Let me see that." She scanned the article while he read over her shoulder. "Because of their friendship with—Oh, Elliott!"

"Jean-Claude Pascal? Isn't he—"

"The chef at the logging camp. The one Lilly apparently worked with at one time. That's what I gathered from the explanation in the Grand Opening menu. This is horrible. We don't want to spotlight a Bonnie-and-Clyde kind of reputation for the inn."

"No. We do not."

"Right. There must be more here. Did they go to jail? Is that why the name changed? What happened to that sweet couple? Help me look."

"They had babies."

"What have you got there?"

"Newspaper gossip column birth announcements clipped together. Looks like Élan and Lilly had four children. No, five. One was stillborn."

"Don't make me cry. So they didn't go to jail. Unless the kids were born before the jewel heist, whatever it was. Elliott!"

"What now?"

Piper clenched her hands and pressed them against her chest. "Jean-Claude Pascal sent the couple a thank-you note."

"That could mean anything. How do you know?"

"It's in my room. I…absconded with it during my last attic escapade. It's addressed to the Lamoreaux couple and signed by Jean-Claude. I'm getting a sick feeling."

"Hang on. This might help. Another headline: 'Logging Camp Chef No Longer Suspect in Theft of Royal Emeralds.'"

"*Royal* Emeralds? This is worse than I thought. Compare the dates of the articles."

"Dated later than the one you have. So obviously, our couple was cleared too. *Hmm.* The article reads, 'Pascal could not be reached for comment. The camp foreman reported Pascal left the logging camp suddenly and without word.'"

"But he was cleared? Our Moose and Butterfly were cleared?"

"It appears so."

They sat in silence, both staring off into an answerless space.

"Are you thinking what I'm thinking?" Piper eventually asked.

"That we should probably figure out what we're having for supper?"

She dropped her head as if her neck had come unhinged. When she raised it, a smile fought its way for dominance on her face. She hummed a few notes. Ah. Clearing her throat. He smiled back.

"I was thinking we should start a spreadsheet to keep all the facts and dates straight. Timelines for what happened when."

"Right after supper. I'm starving. That lumberjack breakfast at lunchtime had no staying power."

"I don't suppose we can get pizza delivery here."

"Better idea. I'll call an order in at the tavern and pick it up while you take a nap."

"The tavern?"

"Best pizza in—"

"In town? That's not great advertising, you know."

"In the county."

"Okay then."

"It'll still be piping hot when I get it home." He reached for his phone. "Good with you?"

"I'm happy to stay in tonight."

"Are you a veggie-only pizza person?"

"Yes. As long as we ask for extra sausage on it."

Elliott chuckled. "Done."

Elliott didn't really think she was going to nap, did he? Not with a metal box full of evidence and potential clues—either to the demise of their plans or the story they'd been searching for.

She readjusted her aching ankle and dove in. Even the Chicago and Milwaukee papers picked up the stories. With an international connection to the crime, it was the hot news of the day. Still, they needed something conclusive.

And it could ruin all hopes of recreating a positive reputation for the inn. How…embarrassing.

Or…they could host mystery weekends and—

No. Where once she was looking for a romantic, intriguing story, she now hoped the one they'd discovered wasn't true.

Her fingers trembled as she held an article written many years later. A small article that reported the emeralds in question had never been found and restored to their original owners—part of France's royal family.

Never recovered. That couldn't bode well for Jean-Claude's innocence. Which reintroduced the possibility of collusion with the darling Moose/Butterfly couple. She dropped her head into her hands. *Elliott, I so wanted to provide a solution for you and your grandmother, not more headaches.*

Maybe he was right. She needed to step away from it for a few minutes. She wouldn't nap, but she could at least prepare something to drink for them. Pizza by candlelight? With real plates and linen napkins? Scratch that. Paper towels. Pizza could get messy.

She'd set the table by the window in the parlor. She didn't know if he needed it, but she needed a moment of serenity in the once-grand building before it was turned over to the bank or some other owner.

Elliott, I tried. I'm sorry. This is not how I hoped it would turn out.

A small voice spoke a different message deep in her heart. *Maybe it's exactly how it should turn out.*

"What are you doing, Piper?"

"Disobeying your grandmother's orders."

"Why?"

"Because you weren't here, and this was just too intriguing."

Elliott slid the pizza box onto the counter. "Something's burning."

"Candles."

"Piper, did you run out of things to investigate?"

"Why do you ask?"

Elliott stared at the apron in Piper's lap. "We had strict instructions not to touch that."

"But then you found a loophole."

"For me. Not for you."

"And then I found a loop-canyon."

"You're making me dizzy."

Piper looked up from her needlework. "Then don't watch. It's probably best if you don't. On second thought, we should eat the pizza while it's hot. I set the table in the parlor. It's a special night."

"In what sense?"

"I found a key in the hem of this apron. Just a few more stitches, and I'll have room to ease it out. Quit changing the subject. Time for pizza. Smells great, by the way."

What could he do but follow her to the candlelit table, holding the pizza box in front of him like a platter of delicacies? He watched, stunned, as she poured sparkling cider into long-stemmed flutes.

"Are we going to talk about any of this?" he asked.

Candlelight danced in her eyes. "I assumed you'd want to say grace first."

Lord God, this woman...

"Was I wrong?"

"No. I already started. Let me continue." He sighed. "Lord God, we thank You for Your goodness to us, for Your unfailing love, for discoveries and"—he opened one eye—"explanations, and for this pizza of which we are about to partake wherewith and henceforth. Amen."

Piper smiled. "You got a little fancy-pants there toward the end, but otherwise...touching. Thank you."

"Speaking of touching aprons, we shouldn't—"

"Technically, not my doing. I believe it was an act of God."

His eyes darted to the ceiling. "Forgive her, Lord, for she knows not what she does."

"I was trying to pull out that step stool in the corner of the kitchen so I could reach the stemware in the butler's pantry. That part went well." She raised her glass as if it was proof.

"Piper Merrill." The image of her balancing on the step stool with a walking boot dangling off to the side made something clench in his heart. Protective versus overprotective. Such a fine line.

"It's when I went to tuck the step stool back where it belonged that things got interesting. I caught the tip of my boot on the leg of the stool and went careening toward an early death…"

"Piper!"

"I grabbed the nearest thing to stabilize myself, which was…"

"The apron." He had to admit she was a good storyteller. And most of it was probably true.

"Which slid off its hook and landed with a clang on the floor."

"A clang?"

"That's what *I* said. 'A clang? What's up with that?' Upon further investigation, I realized there was something sewn into the hem. It wouldn't have been right not to find out what was perhaps stuck there that shouldn't have been."

"Of course." Elliott worked hard not to roll his eyes.

"I'd heard of homemakers sewing weights—like coins or flat rocks—into their apron hems to keep them from flying up when they hung laundry to dry. And sure enough, there were coins or something. But not the last one. I could feel the shape of it. A small key. Like for a safe deposit box, or a padlock, or a…jewelry case."

"Your imagination just took a dangerous detour."

"I know. If the pizza place hadn't been only a couple of blocks away, I might have solved the riddle before you got home. Good pizza, isn't it?"

The rest of my life. I want to spend the rest of my life sitting in the wonder of Piper Merrill's abundance. How can I ever convince her to want the same?

"It's good pizza, yes."

"Elliott." She laid her hand, soft as a butterfly, over his. "I don't want this to end...badly."

She blinked hard.

He could feel his chest heaving but couldn't make it stop.

"We'll keep pursuing clues. Like the key. But if this should wind up hurting you or your grandmother or this inn, I'd never forgive myself."

"That won't happen," he said, resting his other hand on top of hers.

"It could. I don't see how this can end well."

He swallowed. Resisted clearing his throat. "I have one idea."

Her eyes bored into his. "What is it?"

"I'm not currently at liberty to divulge that information."

"Elliott, are we in this together or not?"

"Great question."

The next morning, as she waited for someone to pick up her call, Piper turned the key over in her hands. Old enough to be an antique, that much she knew, but it offered no clues. No safe deposit box-like number engraved in it. No telltale wear marks on its teeth.

The call finally clicked through.

"Hello?"

"Mrs. Cornell. Please don't hang up."

"If this is one of those robot-calls—"

"Robo-calls and no, it isn't. I'm not selling anything. I'd like to talk to your husband, if you don't mind."

"Who is this?"

"I'm Piper Merrill. Elliott Lansing's friend."

"You."

"I understand a little more now why you would want me to stop digging into the past."

The woman paused. "You do?"

"If I could just talk to your husband about when he and his dad worked here on the property."

A sharp intake of breath told Piper that Arlene Cornell was not prepared for that revelation.

"You cannot talk to my husband."

"Please, Mrs. Cornell. It's so important to Elliott's grandmother's future. Has she ever been…unkind to you or your husband?"

The librarian murmured a quiet, "No. Never."

"I have no intention of being unkind either. It's important to know what happened. And I think your husband may be aware of details that will not only help us but will help me avoid accidentally stepping in something that will make your life uncomfortable. I don't want that. I'd like to avoid it."

Silence.

"Mrs. Cornell?"

A loud exhale. "I don't have much time. But I could meet you on Church Street in about fifteen minutes."

"Where on Church Street?" She glanced at her walking boot—as clunky as ever.

"You can see the far end from the near. You won't have trouble finding me."

The call ended.

Church Street. She switched to her navigation app. It ran parallel to Main Street, about a block behind the inn. Elliott was recording a book project. She could be back before he knew she was gone.

∽ Chapter Thirteen ∾

"This stays between us, you hear?" Arlene Cornell crisscrossed the sides of her cardigan over her chest as if it wasn't one of the warmest days they'd had all month. "What happened to your foot?"

So she's not cold and unfeeling. "Twisted my ankle."

"Sorry to hear that."

"May I please have permission to share this with Elliott, and his grandmother?"

"She already knows."

"She does?"

She snorted a little like a horse would when troubled. "You can't talk to my husband, because he's got dementia."

"Oh, Mrs. Cornell. That must be difficult for both of you."

"He's beyond the stage where he's aware what's up and what's down. But out of respect for him is why I hoped you'd stop looking into all of this."

"What happened?"

"My husband was just a teenager. He took a dare, and it cost his father his job at the Moose and Butterfly."

Piper gasped. "You knew it was once called that? How many people in town know?"

"Not even a handful. Wasn't newsworthy after a while. Peggy hadn't taken over the place yet. It was still owned by her parents.

Her mother was a saint, but her dad was as different from her as night and day. Anyway, my Howard took a dare and stole that carving thing. He eventually confessed and all, but Peggy's dad wasn't the forgiving kind. Howard's father lost his job, and that meant they had no place to live either, since they occupied the carriage house on the property."

"Yes, I know. Single father."

"It drove a wedge between those two—Howard Sr. and Howard Jr.—that wasn't resolved before Howard Sr. passed. He was a proud man. A good man. But his integrity kept him from…from showing mercy to his son. Couldn't bear the sight of him. Can you imagine? The shame my husband bore since that day affected everything and everybody around him."

"Including you?"

"He'd 'go dark' sometimes over the rift with his father. Wouldn't come out of it for weeks. And it intensified after his father died. Now, mind you, my husband was just a boy when that happened. And he apologized like he shoulda." She rubbed the green pendant on her necklace chain as if it were a worry stone.

"But if Peggy's parents got the carving back, then why did they—"

"The carving disappeared. Nobody believed my Howard, that he hadn't done something horrid to it or burned it or sold it. He always suspected one of the friends who put him up to swiping it in the first place, but he could never prove it."

"Mrs. Cornell, did Elliott's grandmother commission you to paint a watercolor for her? Was that you?"

"I'd appreciate if you'd keep that between the two of us too. It was kind of a pact between us. A barter. She and I were best friends back when she and her husband first took over the inn. When they thought it would work."

"The inn?"

"And their marriage. We shared a lot in common. Couldn't reach our husbands but for different reasons. One was locked in his selfishness. The other—my Howard—was locked in shame he couldn't shake."

Piper drew a deep breath. "I'm glad you had each other."

"Shortly after I painted that watercolor for her, my Howard put a stop to it. He kept saying it made him feel worse that I was having tea in that inn, making friends with the owner."

"That must have been so hard."

"Excruciating. But there's not much worse for a man shamed than a woman who makes light of it. So we kept our distance, Peggy and me. One of the godliest, kindest women on God's green earth."

Piper imagined Arlene putting brushstrokes to the watercolor paper and her tears making the color spread.

"I made her promise not to mention that moose and butterfly carving again."

Piper reached out to place a hand on Arlene's arm. The woman didn't shake it off. She sighed and almost leaned into the touch.

"That's old history, Mrs. Cornell."

"To some people. Not to my Howard. It's the only memory he hangs on to. I…I don't expect him to live much longer. But until that single memory dies with him, and he's freed of the shame, if this were to get out, or if you were to change the name to the source of his falling out with his father…"

She must have seen my social media post about that possibility. "I understand. I…I wish your Howard knew he could be rid of his shame this side of heaven."

"I do too. He's been stiff-arming God since his dad kicked him out."

"And he doesn't realize God isn't stiff-arming him."

"Right." A tear fell. Then another.

Piper dared reach out to smooth them away. She put her arm around Arlene and let her cry until the woman suddenly pulled away and searched the empty street for onlookers.

"I don't cry much…in public, anyways."

Piper considered her options. Only one seemed reasonable. "I'm confident Elliott will be sensitive to your concerns, Mrs. Cornell. We'll…we'll find some other way to resuscitate the inn."

What that "other way" would be remained the biggest mystery of all.

Log jam.

Piper stared at her laptop screen as she had the past many days. She'd made the French definitions of Embarrass her screen saver. *Bother, perplex, confuse, hamper, clutter, hinder, block, baffle, confound, bewilder, unnerve, entangle* scrolled across her screen. Lovely fonts. Impossible log jam.

They couldn't wish for Howard Jr. to pass. But they couldn't move forward with the name change, logo, website updates, and events without dishonoring a heartbroken woman and a man with only one memory left.

No one knew for sure whether reinstituting the Moose/Butterfly name would even help or be a good move for the inn. Too much remained unanswered about its past. And time was too swiftly ticking by.

Piper and Elliott continued to study in the Situation Room. It was obvious, even in the paperwork, that when the inn passed from Bette Galloway, Lilly's sister, to Élan and Lilly, it came alive with good business sense and marked generosity toward guests and the community as well as those they hired to help. Then, when it passed into Peggy's mother and father's hands, its *joie de vivre* faded. Piper suspected it wasn't the fault of Peggy's mother, the daughter of Élan and Lilly.

Midpage, Elliott pushed his chair back and said, "If a building and business can exhibit zest for life, this one gained it under Lilly and Élan's care and lost it under the management of my great-grandparents. Misuse of funds, mismanagement of resources…"

Piper pondered both the words and the caramel-smooth voice that could make even a pronouncement like that worth listening to. "It's as if Grandma Peggy's father's unforgiveness of Howard Cornell Jr. and his mistreatment and distrust of Howard Sr. set off a pattern of ugliness."

"And it didn't stop when my grandmother inherited it, because of my grandfather's similar habits. It wasn't until my grandfather walked away and left the inn, with all its problems, to Gram's care, that better times came to the inn."

"I have mad respect for that woman. It's a wonder she was able to keep it on life support this long." Piper leaned to rub a shoulder of the man who had chosen to recognize but turn away from the oppression of unforgiveness and follow the branch of his family tree that cared selflessly.

Emboldened by the discoveries they'd made about the toll of secrets and unresolved tensions, Piper took, perhaps, the only opportunity she'd have to get to the heart of Carlton's unusual visits to an inn only a few blocks from his house.

Checking him in on his next traditional reservation day, she held the key to his room an extra moment. "Carlton, do you mind if I ask about your connection to this inn?"

"I suppose anyone would wonder. I wouldn't have done this if the room was needed for other guests."

Piper's confusion must have registered on her face.

"My wife's been bedridden for years. A stroke from which she recovered very little."

"I'm so very sorry."

"She needs total care, around the clock, which I'm honored to give the love of my life."

Piper blinked back tears. A story so different than she'd assumed.

"A couple of years ago," Carlton said, "my wife's sister offered to provide what she calls 'respite' every other week. She spends the day and night with her sister and pays for my room here with tips from her waitressing job at a restaurant in Bonduel. I have a kind person serve me breakfast, I sleep on sheets I don't have to wash, and I remember who I am besides a caregiver. I..."

He paused then went on. "I write my wife love letters while I'm here and read them to her when I go back home."

There it was again—intense love and the power of self-sacrifice.

Piper sat at the kitchen table again watching the *stuck, log jam, entangled* words scroll by and sensing the encroaching nearness of the end of her work assignment with Elliott. She stood, arched her back, and then hobbled to the sink to refresh her glass of water.

Movement caught her eye.

She must have imagined it. Too much screen time.

No, there it was again. How had a mouse gotten into the kitchen? Less creepy than a bat, but not by much.

She grabbed the nearest protective device she could find—the hefty wooden towel rod at the end of the counter. Not the protection she would have hoped for, but the broom was too near where she'd last seen the mouse dart.

"Elliott!"

"Piper!"

His voice came from the backyard. What was he doing out there?

"Elliott! Get in here! Mouse! Not good! Help!"

She brandished the heavier-than-expected towel rod overhead and watched the mouse dart in and out of its hiding places. Under the table, along the cupboards' kickplates, behind the door.

"Elliott!"

When he opened the door from the back hall, the mouse scooted outside between his feet and through the screen door that hadn't yet swung shut.

"I'm here. I'm here," he said. "What in the world?"

"You saw it, didn't you? The mouse?"

"The one that's gone now? That one?"

She drew a deep breath. "Yes. That one. Let's hope he's an introvert who doesn't play well with others."

"What's with the maraca?"

"What?" She still held the weapon overhead. "It's a rolling pin. Or towel rack. It's from there." She pointed to the now empty iron holders in which it once rested.

"Why is it rattling?"

"You cannot blame me for shaking a little. I know mice are small and only carry a few hundred diseases, but…"

"Piper, rolling pins aren't supposed to rattle, are they?" He took it from her hands and shook hard. Muffled, but an unexpected sound.

"It's beautiful. The wood, I mean. Does the end twist off?"

"I don't know."

Elliott put his muscle into it, but Piper stopped him.

"Elliott. Look at that. The engraving. Doesn't that seem familiar to you?"

"Is it supposed to?"

"Give me a minute." Piper returned to her laptop and clicked through to the file of photos Grandma Peggy had sent via email. Hundreds of images. Piper searched for the one that mattered. "There." She tapped the screen.

Elliott leaned in, his breath minty and his deodorant…gone. Completely gone. Replaced by the smell of someone who'd been working hard. "Where have you been?" she asked.

"Piper. The photo?"

"Right. It's the same image."

"Isn't that an unusual coincidence?" He stepped back. A long "*Ohhhh*" reverberated through the air.

"It's exactly the same."

"Did Gram caption that photo—the location or anything?"

"It's labeled 'Culinary museum. Paris. Emblem of renowned chef Auguste Escoffier.'"

"Piper! That's the guy Jean-Claude worked for when the emeralds were stolen from the chef's royal guests at the dinner party at the London Savoy."

"I know."

"But Jean-Claude couldn't have done it. He was exonerated. Wasn't he?"

"That's what we've assumed. Hoped."

More slowly now, Elliott twisted the wooden bulge at the end of the rolling pin. Once it was freed, he tipped the pin over the table. Nothing. "Can I borrow your phone flashlight? Shine it so I can see inside."

She clicked it on for him. "Anything?"

"Can you reach in there? I think there's a piece of cloth in there."

Piper slid out a crumpled piece of disintegrating silk, easing it through the opening. More remained. "Chopsticks. They're the answer to everything."

Elliott grabbed a pair so Piper could pull out more of what had been stuffed within. Something stuck deeper inside finally dislodged and followed the chopsticks out through the opening. "British newsprint and more silk. Looks like it might have once been a scarf. Garishly colored, if you ask me. I think it's an Italian flag." She tugged more. "And—"

Onto the newsprint-covered tabletop tumbled dozens of gems that looked a lot like emeralds.

"They can't be real," Elliott said.

Piper had to take her hand from her gaping mouth to answer. "I think they might be."

A tattered silk scarf and random bits of torn newspaper. Ads and local articles of the time. Nothing about a jewel heist. No hidden clue.

"Does this mean Jean-Claude…"

"Lilly learned so much from Jean-Claude. She highly respected him. He must have given this to her as it had once been given to him."

"Wouldn't she have heard the rolling pin rattle and suspected something?"

"Look at these pieces of newsprint, Elliott. And the remnants of the silk scarf. They were crammed in that cavity. It had to have once been packed so tight no one—likely not even Jean-Claude—knew the rolling pin wasn't solid wood."

"Until now."

"Jean-Claude was basically a pauper, from what it sounds. But he couldn't have been the thief and couldn't have known what was stuffed inside the pin."

"What makes you so sure?"

"Do you think if he had, the man would have handed the honorable rolling pin—and its contents—over to Lilly?"

"Not a chance."

"And Lilly couldn't have known. She was a woman of strong faith, according to what we found in the records. From the Merci note, it appears she assumed she received a thank-you from him that was no more than a couple of French coins and a rolling pin with sentimental value only. She and Élan *couldn't* have known."

"Couldn't have." Elliott's shoulders seemed to relax a little.

"Some of these emeralds are huge." Piper used one of the chopsticks to move them apart.

"I'll be right back."

"You can't leave me with a trillion dollars' worth of stolen emeralds!"

"What are you going to do, Piper? Accidentally swallow one?"

"No, but I might accidentally lose one between the floorboards. You know me."

"I'm just going out the door."

Piper held her breath. "Check first before you open that door. A certain mouse I know may be trying to sneak back in."

"Least of our concerns," Elliott said.

With his back to her, he pulled a wheeled cart up the steps and over the threshold. Covered in heavy canvas, it resembled the shape of a dead body. Knowing Elliott, it was highly unlikely he would wheel a dead body into his grandmother's kitchen. What other explanation…

"I give you," he said, "The Moose and Butterfly." With a flourish, he lifted the canvas off the bulky object.

"I can't believe it! Elliott, it's…just the head."

"The rest of it is outside. Broken in two, right at the neck. But the head is pretty cool." He hoisted it from the wheeled cart and turned it right side up. "Showing its age, but look at that."

Piper was conscious of the irony that she left a massive pile of emeralds to give her attention to a rough carved moose head with a delicate butterfly on its nose. As delicate as wood can be carved. Just like the photos they'd seen, only decapitated.

"Where did you find this?"

"The key from the apron kept bugging me. What other lock hadn't we tried? It occurred to me there's a funny lock on the shed out back. Remember when I was looking for a ladder to take care of Harvey the squirrel in the attic?"

"I do."

"Couldn't budge that unusual lock on the shed, but I found the ladder hanging on the back side of the shack, so I didn't give it much thought. That's why no one's used the shed for years, I suppose."

"And this was sitting right there all along?"

"Under a pile of hundred-year-old lumber. It took more than a little effort to move it all. Somebody didn't want the carving found. Not for a long while anyway. And I discovered it like this—in two pieces."

"Howard returned it? When?"

"Or Howard's dad did."

"*Ooh*."

"Howard's dad might have had it all along but was trying to teach his son a lesson."

"That's harsh. And unlikely. He lost his job over it."

"True. We may never know."

Piper studied the carving. She ran her fingers over the grooves and dips, the antlers, the nose, the somehow gossamer butterfly wings made of solid wood. "Elliott. El-li-ott, did you look at this butterfly's eyes?"

"I did. Green."

"Uh huh. One might say *emerald* green."

"And one is missing."

CHAPTER FOURTEEN

An hour later, they both sat at the kitchen table again, elbows on its surface, chins resting in their cupped hands.

"It was here all along. Every time your grandmother did dishes, she was inches away from this inconceivable wealth."

Elliott sighed. "Hard to fathom, isn't it? Do you think she knew? Knows?"

Piper matched his sigh. "I think she knew about the romance between Élan and Lilly, and she knew about the carving. It's what connected her to them—the love she wished she'd experienced. The love that marked this inn ages ago."

"The watercolor."

"Right. I think she fiercely believed in the power of a love that endures, even though she hadn't seen it in her parents or her own marriage. Or her daughter's. But if she'd known about the carving's return, I'm confident she would have told Arlene. I can't imagine your grandmother knew about the rolling pin. The carving and the rolling pin are only connected circumstantially, right?"

"Why would she insist we not touch the apron? She must have been aware of the key in its hem, and what it belonged to. Did she suspect? Not want us to find it? Or did she count on our curiosity winning out over her warning? Did she *intend* us to figure it out?"

"Elliott, she's an honest woman. A little quirky, but who isn't?"

He turned to her at that.

"She would have reported a haul of gems like this. But there would have been no reason to tell the authorities that the carving was back home. No charges were ever filed, were they?"

"Don't know."

Elliott returned his chin to his cupped hands. "I wonder what happened to the butterfly's missing eye."

"We're not even sure that the glass in this butterfly eye is the same as—Okay, same deep green color. Granted."

"We've spent a lot of hours in this kitchen. All the times I visited here, I never suspected that towel holder was more than what it appeared to be."

Piper laughed then sobered. "We have three calls to make, don't we?"

"Yup."

"Mrs. Cornell—so she can tell her Howard that the carving has been found and it's where it belonged. We won't tell her it needs a little repair work. Then your grandmother, to tell her about, well, everything, and ask her a few pointed questions. Then the police, to see how we locate the descendants of the original owners of these gems."

"I wouldn't have listed them in that order, but yes. Although..."

"What?"

"When word reaches the police, it'll reach the news, and that will bring all kinds of attention to this place."

Piper lifted her head from her hands. "You're not talking about keeping this find a secret."

"No. No. But I wonder how we can stave off the attention until the gems are returned to their owners or the estate or whatever."

"You do realize we've worked for weeks to try to find a way to draw attention to the inn."

"Well aware."

"And that we're sitting on a pretty big story."

"Also aware."

"And that we're probably going to be guilty of something if we delay informing the police. And that if something happens to these emeralds while they're in our possession…"

"I know a fairly decent hiding place for them."

"Elliott!"

One call at a time. One step at a time.

Gram seemed shocked, pleased, and distracted rolled into one. She'd kept the metal box of newspaper items locked, she said, because she wanted, with everything within her, to believe that Élan and Lilly were innocent. And it seemed they were, since if they'd known about the gems, they never would have left the rolling pin right there in the open all those years. It hadn't become a nest egg they left to their children. They'd struggled like anyone else…but found joy in the process.

And shocked? Yes. How many times had she grabbed a towel from that rod, never suspecting it wasn't solid wood?

Over speakerphone, Gram admitted she knew about the key in the apron, had even peeked into the shed a time or two, but had no idea it was the carving's hiding place all those years.

"I made a solemn promise to Arlene not to bring up the subject," she said. "I couldn't go back on my word and ask someone to go hunting for it. But if a person I trusted stumbled onto it... With Howard the way he is now, I wanted so much for Arlene's heart to be at peace and for you to know that this inn hasn't always been as it is now. Or was the generation before me."

"You broke the pattern, Gram," Elliott said.

"I admit my fascination with the love story of Élan and Lilly became a bit of an obsession for me. Yes, I sewed the embroidery in the pockets and left it hanging in the kitchen as a symbol—mostly to myself, I guess—that sometimes love does work. It doesn't always disappoint."

Piper chimed in. "Grandma Peggy, the eyes in the butterfly?"

"What about them?"

"One's missing."

"Oh, that's a shame."

Piper held her breath. *We're not talking about the same kind of shame, Gram.* "The eyes are green stones or glass or... Could it be...?"

"Could it be what, dear?"

"The one still in place looks like..."

Gram's sharp intake of breath traveled halfway around the globe. Elliott calmed her. "We'll have it analyzed with the rest."

"Oh, dear. This could be a bit of an issue. One's missing? I'm not cut out for prison. And I have plans."

Gram suddenly announced she had to hang up. Despite the enormity of their news, Piper and Elliott apparently had to take a back seat to whatever excursion Gram was embarking on with Evelyn and the friends they'd met on the trip. Gram gave Elliott her full permission to handle the findings as he saw fit.

"Oh," she added, "I should have told you sooner, Elliott, dear. I'm asking you again. If you want the inn, it's yours. If I'm not behind bars, I'm getting married as soon as we get back. He's a wonderful man. We're moving—to a larger city than Embarrass, Wisconsin."

Elliott leaned closer to the phone. "Gram, are you sure about this?"

"It's not all that sudden. My beloved is Evelyn's brother. We've been friends for years. He's proposed four or five times in the past, but I always turned him down. I didn't think I deserved a love like that. I was wrong. It took this trip with him and our ever-vigilant chaperone Evelyn to convince me."

"I'm stunned. But happy for you."

"I understand if you don't want the inn. I'm kind of saddling you with an albatross."

"A butterfly, Gram."

"I hope you two will be pleased to know we won't be living that far away. I'm moving from Embarrass, Wisconsin, to Embarrass, Minnesota. Much larger. Population of almost 700."

Piper's second thoughts about informing Mrs. Cornell right away resonated with Elliott. Howard wouldn't be able to comprehend. And if he did, he might wonder if his father had been even more cruel and unforgiving than Howard Jr. realized. The ripples of unforgiveness still rolled through that family, and the discovery wouldn't do anything to stop them.

They agreed, though, that contacting the authorities in France first might be the most prudent path. The theft had occurred in

England, but the guests were French royalty. The French authorities would have direct access to the information needed to locate the original owners. They also agreed they might need a lawyer's advice and his or her presence during the call. Who knew there was a French consulate in Chicago? Their offices proved invaluable in directing them to the precise people in France who would handle the case.

Piper stared into the fire they'd lit in the fireplace on an unusually cool, rainy night. Elliott's arm rested just above her shoulders on the back of the couch. "Elliott, did you for even a moment think about not reporting the emeralds? In a way, they would have been the answer to a lot of financial concerns."

"Not for a second."

"That's another thing I love about you. Your integrity."

"You…used the word *love*."

Her throat tightened. "I love mango ice cream. I love the sound of your voice. That kind of love."

"That's what you meant?"

She turned her face to his. "No. That's not what I meant." It was now or never. If he didn't feel as she did, at least she would have been honest with him. "I meant this kind." She stretched to kiss him briefly on the lips.

"I see. Well, that changes things. I don't think it's any mystery how I feel about you."

She pulled back a few inches. "Yes, it is. It's a mystery. I'm not sure how you feel. I know you tolerate me quite well."

At that, he laughed—a deep, glorious laugh that wiggled the flames in the fireplace. "Piper, I adore you. I can't imagine my life or this place without you in it. I thought you were better at picking up clues." He drew her into his embrace.

She listened for a long time to the sound of his heartbeat before she reached up and kissed him again.

It had taken almost two months to arrange and a few extra narration gigs to pay for it, but the look on Piper's face was worth it all as the hot-air balloon lifted off the ground.

"Is it as magical as you imagined?" he asked when they'd reached a cruising altitude and the balloon could float in relative silence without the blast of the flames.

"Even more. Elliott, what made you decide to do this for me?"

"Two things. When I mentioned Gram had been on a hot-air balloon ride once, you said it sounded like fun."

"You remembered that?"

"And the second thing is because I thought it would make a memorable place for me to propose." He knelt awkwardly in the basket of the balloon and extended an open ring box to her.

"Elliott, it's beautiful!"

"An emerald-cut diamond. I hoped you'd like it."

"I would have been happy with the green bottle glass from the non-missing butterfly eye."

Elliott drew back the ring box. "I could arrange that."

"Not on your life! I love it. This kind of love." She bent to kiss him. The toe of her shoe caught on a rope, and she tumbled into his arms.

As the balloon slowly descended, Piper noticed a black limo parked beside her rental car in the lot. "Elliott, you didn't. A limo? That's so not us."

"No. I didn't. I don't know what that's about."

When Elliott and Piper approached on foot, a man leaning against the limo stood tall and nodded to them.

"*S'il vous plaît, pardonnez-moi.* You are Mr. Elliott Lansing?"

"Yes. How can I help you?"

"It is my pleasure to inform you of the gratitude of my clients on the return of their family treasure."

"Oh my." Piper pressed a sparkling hand to her heart.

Elliott extended his hand to the stranger. "There was no need to come so far. I…we are grateful that we were able to locate your clients and make the exchange."

"You may be unaware that, despite the many years that have passed, a reward for the return of the jewels has been kept in trust all this time."

"There's no need for that. Returning them was the right thing to do."

"I believe you will, as they say, exchange your mind when you realize the interest that has accumulated over a hundred years." The man reached into his suitcoat pocket and retrieved an envelope.

Elliott waved Piper closer and opened the note tucked inside.

"The money will be deposited in the account of your choice via wire exchange after you contact the number in the note and of course offer proof of identity. *Bonsoir.* Good day."

Elliott and Piper stood where they were, staring at the message long enough for the sun to remind them spring was turning into summer.

"Elliott?"

"Yes?"

"That's what I'd call an embarrassment of riches."

Dear Reader,

We hope you've enjoyed your visit to Embarrass, Wisconsin, both past and present. When we were presented with the opportunity to write about this small historic community, we immediately planned to meet there for a "research" trip. (Quotation marks are needed, since we have way too much fun on these trips to justify calling it real work.) On our visit to the town with a name that means "obstruction," God provided several breakthroughs, including meeting, like Piper, a postmistress with a folder passed on to her by the previous postmistress that contained a goldmine of historical information. We also visited the Menominee Logging Museum and took tons of pictures that helped us visualize Lilly saving the town and falling in love with her Moose.

Authors are often asked where they find inspiration for their characters. Since one cardinal rule is to not make our characters too perfect, our own flaws can offer a wealth of possibilities. Like Lilly, learning not to jump ahead of God is a struggle for many of us. If you've also had occasion to embarrass yourself by making knee-jerk assumptions, you may have felt a true kinship with Lilly. She has a big heart and loves life, but her enthusiasm sometimes lands her in awkward situations. It's fun to imagine her a few years into her future, hopefully just as fun but a bit less impetuous, as she and Élan parent their four children and serve their guests and the community together.

Elliott and Piper's story had the joy of living in the legacy Élan and Lilly left, but theirs is a journey of their own. Piper's exuberance for life and Elliott's quiet demeanor might have made them polar opposites, but it's soon obvious they're perfect for each other, quirks and all. Where once they might have thought making a name for themselves—and the town—was a worthy and necessary goal, like many of us they come to realize and celebrate the truth that it's in sacrificing for others that we find what we were truly looking for all along.

We authors conferred on basics, but until we saw each other's final files, we didn't know how many details our two couples— 120 years apart—shared in common but expressed in completely different ways. We hope you had fun discovering those "gems" as you read both stories.

A story circle isn't complete until readers hold the book in their hands. We're grateful for you!

Love,

Becky and Cynthia

∽ About the Authors ∽

Becky Melby

Becky Melby has written or coauthored twenty-six fiction titles, including numerous Guidepost cozy mysteries. She is a weekly devotional blogger on social media at Fill My Cup, Lord. Becky and Bill, her husband of fifty years, call Wisconsin home. They are the parents of four sons and have fifteen grandchildren. When not writing or spending time with family, Becky may be found riding on the back of their Honda Gold Wing motorcycle or touring the country in their motorhome.

Cynthia Ruchti

Cynthia Ruchti's writing journey began as many do, with an article here and a blog post there. Then she wrote short fiction and devotions for a radio broadcast that became a three-decade-long ministry on the air. Since 2010 when she released her first novel, she's published almost 40 works of fiction and nonfiction, including contributing to Guidepost's *Mornings with Jesus* daily devotionals since 2014. Cynthia and her grade-school-sweetheart husband live in the heart of Wisconsin, not far from their three children and six (to date) grandchildren. Her tagline is "I can't unravel. I'm hemmed in Hope."

Story Behind the Name

Embarrass, Wisconsin

Embarrass may be an unpleasant, cringe-worthy emotion, but it's also the name of a small village in the eastern part of Wisconsin, not far from Green Bay. A writer's imagination could invent all kinds of creative stories for how a town could come to be known by a name like that. A clothesline full of woodsmen's thermal underwear hanging on the line during its lumber days. A blushing mayor's wife when her hat blew into the fireworks display on the day Embarrass incorporated. An unfortunate typo in important legal documents that was never rectified.

The true story, as best as can be determined by the little written about it, is that the village was named for the Embarrass River that runs through it. Kind of like the elephant in the room. *If a river named Embarrass runs through the town, we might as well quit trying to ignore it and just name the town for it.*

But the background has—appropriately enough for our stories—a romantic thread running through it too, if you think anything said with a French accent is romantic.

When the timber industry was thriving in that part of Wisconsin, French Canadian voyageurs, explorers, and woodsmen passed through or migrated to the area. They brought tools and skills and a French "flavor" to the lumber trade. And they brought a unique perspective on the twisted, double-back, bottlenecked river they found was difficult to navigate and often a source of log jams as they floated logs to the lumbermills downstream. They called it *Rivière d'Embarras,* which some translate from the French as "River of Obstacles."

The characters in both the historical and contemporary stories in *Love's a Mystery in Embarrass, Wisconsin,* found that the name fits well.

Lilly's Coffee-Chocolate Chess Pie

Ingredients:

Crust (Or use Grandma Peggy's premade crust shortcut):

2 cups flour

½ teaspoon salt

2 tablespoons sugar

11 tablespoons butter, chilled and cut into small cubes

4–5 tablespoons ice water

For the filling:

1½ cups sugar

3 eggs

5 ounces heavy cream

1 teaspoon vanilla

3 tablespoons cocoa

2 tablespoons strong black coffee

Topping:

Sweetened whipped cream

Instructions:

1. For piecrust, mix together flour, salt, and sugar in bowl of stand mixer with paddle attachment. With mixer running, slowly add butter cubes one by one until mixture resembles coarse meal. Add tablespoons of water one at a time until mixture comes together.

2. Let dough cool for about 30 minutes in the refrigerator, then roll out and shape in 8- or 9-inch pie pan.

3. For filling, whisk together all ingredients until well combined. Pour into unbaked pie shell. Bake 30 minutes in oven preheated to 350 degrees or until dough is lightly golden and center of custard is set. Let cool.

4. Top with sweetened whipped cream.

Read on for a sneak peek of another exciting book
in the Love's a Mystery series!

Love's a Mystery *in*
Whynot, North Carolina
by Emily Quinn & Laura Bradford

Love's Sweet Memories
By Emily Quinn

Whynot, North Carolina
September 1965

Madeline Alice Kircher closed her suitcase. As she looked around her small apartment, she picked up a sweater she wanted to take as well. Packing for a week of cleaning and boxing up her father's household shouldn't be this hard. The phone rang, and she detoured back into the kitchen, where it hung on the wall. She turned off the radio that was playing the Beatles' newest song, "Help."

"This is Maddie Kircher, can I help you?"

"Well, isn't that a professional greeting. Your dad was always so proud of the life you made there in the big city." A rough but kind voice filled her ear.

"Sorry, Mr. Lane, I rarely get calls at home. How have you been?" Maddie sat on the chair she had positioned under the phone just for this situation. Her long legs stuck out in front of her, dressed in lime green capris and matching green flats. At five-nine, she didn't need to add any height to her slim frame. Thomas Lane was her father's best friend. Or had been. She still couldn't believe he was gone.

"I'm good, Maddie. And call me Thomas, please. I'm missing Max, but that's to be expected still, right? Your dad's passing was so sudden, but at least he's reunited with your blessed mother. Anyway, I don't want to spend time on that. Phone calls aren't cheap. I was just calling to make sure you'll be here this weekend." Thomas Lane didn't waste any time on small talk. Especially not on a long-distance call.

"I'm leaving early tomorrow morning and will be there by midday. I can stay in the apartment until Thursday, right?" Maddie reached for the notebook where she'd written all the tasks she needed to do while she was in Whynot. She needed to be back at her desk at nine a.m. next Friday, a week from tomorrow, which meant she had a busy week ahead of her.

A picture of her mom hung on the wall in her living room. Her mother's blue eyes and blond hair made the picture almost a mirror for Maddie, except Maddie had her father's strong mouth and chin. She didn't have one picture of her mom where she wasn't smiling. Maddie's own photo history was not as happy as her mother's.

"The new owner takes possession on Wednesday, so you'll have to talk to him about the last night. We have a guest room at our house you can use if you need a place to stay." Thomas was also her father's attorney and had handled the sale of the building that held the Whynot Café as well as the apartment above it, where Maddie's family had lived since she was born. And where her father had been living until he died in a car accident. "I know this is hard for you, coming back after losing him. But he loved you. Lots."

"Tomorrow I'll start work to get the building cleared out." Maddie had made a list of the things she wanted to bring back to Raleigh. The list included her mother's wedding china, some crystal glassware, the family Bible, and the piano. She was sure she'd find more things she couldn't part with, so she was going prepared. Her car was packed with boxes she'd gotten from the local grocery store last weekend. Of course, she'd have to make special arrangements to move the piano.

"Then we can talk when you get here. Come over to the house, and Ethel and I will feed you. She's planning on frying a chicken and baking your mom's favorite peach pie."

After Maddie hung up, she made a note to remind herself to have dinner with the Lanes. They'd been part of her life since she could remember. Of course, there were a lot of Whynot residents who'd been there day after day at the café.

Maddie tried to push aside the memories of her mom and Aunt Alice singing at the piano on Saturday night with the whole dining room singing along. She'd watch her father standing at the door of the kitchen smiling while he listened. Tears stung her eyes.

She went to the fridge to see what she had left that she needed to use up before her trip. She'd take anything she wouldn't eat to her neighbor, Elisa, next door. With three kids, there was always too much month left at the end of their money.

Maddie found cheese, milk, and some leftover ham to make a macaroni and cheese bake. She cooked, she turned on the radio and hummed along to her favorite songs as she cooked. Elvis always had a sadness to his tone. Her mom would say he sang from the heart.

After dinner, she cleared out her refrigerator and took the perishables, including the leftover macaroni and cheese, to her neighbor's apartment. As she carried the food to Elisa's kitchen, one of the kids climbed up on a stool.

"Mama, can we have that for dinner?" He pointed to the casserole dish.

Elisa blushed as she put the dish into the oven to reheat. "I haven't cooked anything yet. Steve is working late."

"Well then I'm glad I had leftovers. I just can't seem to cook for one person." Maddie placed the milk inside Elisa's nearly empty icebox.

"I still can't believe you're moving your dad's things all by yourself." Elisa took a book from her toddler as he held it up to her. "Thank you, George."

Elisa grinned at the chaos going on around her. "And I can't believe you wrangle these three kids all day. We each have our gifts."

"It's not the same, and you know it." Elisa picked up George, put him on her hip, and wiped his face with a dish towel. "He's teething."

"I better get home and finish packing. I'll see you next weekend." Maddie paused as she walked to the door. "Can I bring you something from my father's house? Blankets? Pots and pans?"

"Oh, we're fine. If you come across something you think I could use, like maybe some books, I'd appreciate it." Elisa kissed little George on the forehead. "But we're fine."

When Maddie got back to her apartment, she wrote Elisa's name on the list, just to remind herself to be on the lookout. The young family had a lot of love in their two-bedroom apartment, but not a lot else.

Maddie walked through her rooms, cleaning and putting things away while she tried to slow down her mind so she could fall asleep. Finally, she shut off the lights and headed to bed. Tomorrow was going to come no matter what. She needed to be well rested for the trip.

Friday at noon, Austin Grant pulled his old truck into the parking lot of what used to be the Whynot Café. He unfolded his six-foot-two-inch frame out of the driver's seat and stretched his legs. "Hey Spot, come on out, we're home."

His large black lab jumped out of the truck and sniffed around the aging building. Austin went over to the side of the property where a grove of trees lined the lot and tried to peer through the dirt-encrusted windows. The first room was a large dining area filled with wooden tables. It looked like someone had closed the door after a night shift and just not come back. Salt and pepper shakers still sat on the tables, which were covered with faded red-and-white tablecloths. A small stage area took up one side of the rear wall, and there was a lunch counter in front of where the kitchen must be. He really wanted to get inside again and see the kitchen.

When he'd purchased the building, he'd only had one walk-through. The price had been right for an as-is property, but since he was signing the paperwork and the next thirty years of his life away, he worried about everything. From the condition of the kitchen appliances to the building's foundation and even the presence of termites. He never knew there were so many things to consider when buying a building. Everyone at his last job had at least one horror story to tell the soon-to-be restaurateur.

"This is what you wanted, so deal with it," he mumbled to himself. He'd been trying to think positive since he'd left Atlanta yesterday. Now, he was thinking the building where he was going to start his new life was less of a great buy and more of a horrible money pit.

He circled the building, looking in the windows as much as they allowed, and tried not to panic. Spot's barking brought him out of his bad mood, and he ran back to the parking lot, expecting his dog to have found a rabbit, or worse, a turtle. Spot hated turtles.

Spot was at the front door, sniffing and barking. He had seen what Austin hadn't. The door was ajar. He pushed it open wider and scanned the dimly lit dining room. A crash sounded to his left. Someone or something was in the building. He glanced around for something to use as a weapon, but all he could find was an old umbrella in a stand by the door. At least he had a good swing from his years playing pickup baseball games.

He motioned for Spot to sit and stay, and the dog whined, not willing to let his owner go into danger alone. But if it was a racoon, or worse, a bear, he didn't want Spot in the middle of a fight he couldn't win. Austin would know to run for the truck. Spot would prefer the fight. Maybe he should lock Spot in the truck before—

Another crash. Whatever was in there would have the place torn up before he could get Spot to safety.

He left Spot outside to guard the entrance. Hopefully, Austin could open another door and get the animal to leave through that. He moved quietly through the dining room, keeping close to the walls. When he got to the swinging doors of the kitchen, he peeked inside.

Then he lowered the umbrella and stepped into the kitchen, staring at a pretty young woman picking up pans from the floor.

"Can I help you?" He leaned against a wall.

When she saw him, she grabbed a saucepan and held it up like a weapon.

"Hey, whoa there," he exclaimed. "You're the one trespassing in my building. Who are you?"

"This isn't your building. It's…" She paused, and Austin sensed she changed the words she was going to use. "My father's café. At least until the sale is finalized. What are you doing here, and why are you holding an umbrella?"

Austin blinked and looked at the makeshift weapon in his hand. He nodded to her upheld pan. "I'll put down my weapon if you'll put down yours."

"You haven't told me who you are." She raised the saucepan higher.

"Sorry, you're right. I'm Austin Grant. I purchased this building a couple of weeks ago. The final walk-through and closing are on Wednesday. I came in early. I'm working with Thomas Lane on the sale." He set the umbrella in the corner. He could still reach it if she was determined to attack, but he'd gone this far in life without hitting a woman, and he hoped she wouldn't force his hand.

The woman blinked and let out a long breath, the arm holding the pan dropping to her side. She set it on the counter. "I didn't realize you were already here. I thought I'd have more time. I'm Madeline Kircher. Maddie. I grew up here, and now I'm the owner of the building. Ever since my dad passed last month."

"I'm so sorry for your loss." Austin had known the owner was deceased, but he didn't realize he had a daughter. Especially one so pretty. The smell of lemon bars filled the kitchen. "I'd like to look around, if that's okay."

A door slammed open, and Spot ran into the kitchen. The dog came to a sliding stop when he saw Maddie. He looked up at Austin and licked his hand. "I guess I didn't close the door tight enough."

"Is that your dog?" She juggled her purse on her shoulder, not moving from her place by the window.

"This is Spot. He's a sweetheart." He waved her over to where they stood. "Thomas said someone would be around clearing out the place until the contracts are signed. We might as well get acquainted. Let Spot sniff the back of your hand."

"Seriously? I'm not completely sure you're not an intruder." She stood, watching them watch her. Finally, she stepped closer and tentatively held out her hand, keeping her fingers curled to her palm. Spot sniffed her hand then licked it, looking up at her with a big doggy smile. "He's cute, but why is he named Spot? He doesn't have a bit of white on him at all."

Austin grinned. "Exactly. He's one big black spot. So how did you get inside? Did Thomas come and let you in? I was supposed to go to his office and get a key when I got into town, but since I was passing by, I thought I might as well stop and look around first."

She ignored his questions and scrutinized him closely. "Why did you buy the Whynot Café? Are you from the area?"

"I'm from Atlanta. At least that was the last place I lived." He felt like he was being interviewed for a job he didn't want. As he watched, the woman walked out of the kitchen and over to the front door of the café. He followed her outside as she pointed to a large planter that had an overgrown rosemary plant growing inside.

"Ever since I was little, Dad had a hidey hole right here for a key." She held up a key. "Ta-dah! Now, Mr. Grant, let me show you what you bought and see if you still want to go through with the deal."

They wandered back inside the dark room. If the windows hadn't been covered with dirt, the room might seem sunny. He flipped the switch by the door, and light flooded the room. Some of the fixtures had broken bulbs, but most of them worked. He blew out a breath. This was doable. He was starting to believe he could actually pull off an opening sometime next month, with a little luck and a whole lot of elbow grease. "How long has it been shut down?"

"I'm not sure." She stopped scanning the room and walked back to the lunch counter. "I loved watching my mom make milkshakes here. I'd sit on that stool after school, and she'd make me one while I did my homework."

Not exactly the information he was looking for, but a nice reminiscence. The woman—Maddie, he corrected himself—seemed to be on her own personal walk down memory lane. Austin went back into the kitchen and found another set of light switches. He flipped them on, and a cat hissed in the corner. Spot came to attention by Austin's side. Austin felt Maddie walk by him and realized the smell of lemon bars was coming from her. "Is that a stray? How did he get inside?"

"A stray? No, that's T Rex. Thomas told me that Dad's cat was still around. He tried to catch him, but apparently, he's very comfortable here. I can take him home with me but not until next month when I move into my new house in Raleigh. It's a rental, but the landlord has already approved me for a pet." She went over and picked up the large gray cat. He leaned into her like he was butter.

"He seems to like you. I guess he can hang around until you return. I don't care. Spot might have strong feelings about sharing his new home, but I'll watch out for him. T Rex, huh? Like the dinosaur?"

Maddie laughed, and the sound echoed in the empty building. "Yes, my dad was an amateur paleontologist. He was very disappointed when I didn't go to school to get a degree in that field. He and I both had strong feelings about my future."

"He sounds interesting. I'm sorry I didn't meet him." Austin went over to check out the stove and grill. As long as they still worked, he wouldn't have to buy new ones. The refrigerator, that was another story. He examined the floor around it and found evidence of leakage. As he checked the storage area, he asked her again when the diner was last open. When he got no answer, he looked up and saw she'd moved to the dining room. He watched as she paced from one side to another, searching for something.

"It's not here." She pulled out a chair and sat down, her hair in her eyes. "I can't believe it."

Austin lowered himself next to her with Spot by his side. He could feel the woman's pain. "What's not here?"

"A piano. It was an old upright that my mom used to play. Maybe it's upstairs in the apartment." She rubbed the cat's ears. "If you're done down here, we can go up and look. Is there going to be a problem with me staying in my old room in the apartment until next Thursday?"

"You want to stay in the apartment after we sign? I was hoping, since it's vacant, to ask if there was any way I could stay here until the contract's signed. I guess Spot and I can sleep down here on a cot or something." He blushed and, for a minute, felt like a shy kid in high school. "Unless there's a motel nearby."

"No motel. I'll stay in the apartment packing up stuff, and you can have the downstairs until I leave. Thank you." She stood and brushed the dust off her pants. "Let's go up to the apartment and see if the piano's there."

"I don't think they'd move a piano upstairs," Austin said, but he realized Maddie hadn't heard him. She had already walked over to a doorway that led to a narrow hall. He followed her.

She passed by the bathrooms and opened a door at the end of the hallway. It had a faded sign on the door that read EMPLOYEES ONLY. "You may want to get a lock for this. People keep thinking it's a bathroom."

He followed her up the narrow dust-covered stairs. So far, the place just needed a good cleaning—as long as the fridge was usable. A bucket of water and a few gallons of Pine-Sol should be effective. Well, several buckets of water. The walls were covered with dirt and grime. *That's why I got a good price*, he reminded himself.

Austin was happy that the apartment was a nice size with three bedrooms and a full bath. The kitchen upstairs had been updated since the original build, and Austin could see from the condition of the upscale appliances that the former owner had a love of cooking. He could tell right away which room was Maddie's by the pink color explosion. He met her as he returned to the living room, a huge smile on his face. "I can't believe how much space this has just for me and Spot. I'm used to renting a room. It's easier when you're working at a restaurant most of the time."

"What did you do with Spot when you worked? Did he stay in your room?" Maddie asked, picking a book up off a pile and thumbing through it as they talked.

"Mostly he hung at the back of the restaurant or in the truck. He's pretty attached. I hated that I didn't have a yard for him to run in, but we'd stop at the park before we went to work." Austin felt guilty that Spot hadn't had a normal home, but he'd found the pup wet and shivering in the cold outside the restaurant one night. He'd been planning on finding the guy a home, but he'd never had the time. And, he had to admit to himself, he really hadn't wanted to give him away to someone else. So, Spot had stayed. Now, he needed to figure out where his new property line ended so he could give Spot his own green space. And maybe add a small grill and a picnic table. Man, he was sounding like a suburban dad or something. Definitely not the wild child who'd left home after graduation and crisscrossed the country earning his cooking chops. His mom would be proud of this version of her son.

"I never had a pet of my own since I left home. I mean, I had cats as a kid, but when I left, well, the apartment I rented didn't allow pets. I'm moving to a house next month, and my landlord allows small pets." She set the book down. "And I already told you that. I guess I'm tired from the drive."

Austin glanced around the apartment, not willing to stop exploring yet. Or was it something else—or someone else—he wasn't willing to leave? "Your dad was a bit of a collector, wasn't he?"

Maddie nodded and swept her hand around the living room full of books on every flat spot and stacked up the walls. "It looks like he tried to keep everything. Except the one thing I wanted most of all. It's gone!"